30-Day Change in Me

1 CHANGE EVERY 30 DAYS TO FIND FREEDOM AND LIVE LIFE TO THE FULLEST

LAURA ORTEGA

30-Day Change in Me by Laura Ortega

Published by Laura Ortega in Lewisville, Texas

Library of Congress Control Number: 2021903711

Visit the Author's Website at ***30daychangeinme.com***

For permissions, contact: 30daychangeinme@gmail.com

Cover by Les Germancreative (@Germancreative)
Cover photo by @jovanniortega
Cover font from elements.envato.com
Editor: Abbey Espinoza and Lindsey Duffy
Scripture Design: Lorena Nuñez
Interior Design and Layout: Md Waheduzzaman Manik

ISBN: 978-1-7354726-1-4

This book is dedicated to Jovanni, the love of my life, who was instrumental in the success of the challenges, and continues to encourage me to be faithful to the projects God gives me to complete. I love you to the moon and back.

30 Day Change in Me

Commit your actions to the Lord and your plans will succeed

Proverbs 16:3

THE LAUNCH

Have you ever embarked on a journey without knowing where it would lead? An idea comes to your mind seemingly out of nowhere, but it won't leave your head. You can't shake it. It grows and blossoms inside of you, and you want to blurt out the news to everyone you know: "God's given me a project! I don't know any of the details yet, but I'm brimming with excitement just thinking about the possibilities!"

That's how 30-Day Change in Me was born. I was on the treadmill one day, praying as I fought the desire to quit mid-stride. I had felt so stuck that week. I needed a breakthrough, and longed to experience God's freedom again in the area of eating and self-control. Earlier that same day, I had made a commitment to get myself back on track. I decided to pursue a month-long journey of eating no processed foods, and no dairy or wheat either. This plan is more commonly known as the "Clean Eating" challenge. I had done a Clean Eating before with friends, and I loved how much energy I had while doing it. I desperately needed that fresh start—but I also knew I needed accountability. So many times in my life, I had started programs like this only to stop, leaving them incomplete. Through those experiences, I learned that I'd never make it relying on my own strength.

And that's when the idea hit me. The concept of the "Clean Eating" challenge was to remain consistent for thirty days in order to make a lifestyle change. What would my life look like a year from now if I decided to make one intentional change to my life every thirty days, and truly stuck to it? Like many of you, I had experienced years of failed resolutions, starting over each Monday in an endless cycle. But thirty days... Could I keep a goal for just thirty days straight? Sure! That sounded a lot more manageable and achievable to my scatterbrained life.

Then, after the 30 days of complete, uncompromising consistency were over, I could reflect and evaluate the long-term changes I would want to make to my life based on that month's experience. What newly established routines would I decide to incorporate into my daily schedule? What did I learn about myself, God, and others that would spur me on toward becoming a better version of myself and walking in my purpose?

But hold on. If I were to do this, and really commit to these thirty-day challenges, I would need two essential things:

1. God's help. Proverbs 16:3 says, "Commit your

actions to the LORD, and your plans will succeed" (NLT)[1].

2. Accountability. Hebrews 10:24-25 reminds me, "And let us consider how to stir up one another to love and good works, not neglecting to meet together, as is the habit of some, but encouraging one another, and all the more as you see the Day drawing near" (ESV)[2].

God is faithful. So I knew for sure, if this idea had truly come from Him, He would bless it and help me. For accountability, I began to look to social media. I had seen several people posting workouts and follow-along routines via their social media stories, saw how they received encouragement and, in turn, inspired others in their fitness journeys.

My heart was stirring: "What if people could follow along or join in on these thirty-day challenges? What difference would it make in our lives?"

> ***What if we as Christ-followers truly began living the abundant life that Jesus promised in John 10:10b?***[3]

---

[1] Holy Bible: New Living Translation. Wheaton, Illinois: Tyndale House Publishers, 2004. Print.

[2] ESV Study Bible: English Standard Version. Wheaton, Illinois: Crossway Bibles, 2007. Print

[3] "I came that they may have life and have it abundantly." (ESV

Think about the freedom we'd experience–the witness we would be to the world!

So, I invite you now to step into this journey of freedom and abundance with me as I share with you each 30-Day Change in Me challenge.

At the end of each chapter are some reflection questions to kick-start your journey. You can also visit my social media pages[4] where you can see live footage of the transformation I was experiencing when I first did these challenges, and the lessons God taught me. You'll also find a code to join our social media tribe (30daychangeinme) to help you with each challenge in the back of the book.

But before we begin, I need you to know something. Lasting change is not something you can accomplish in your own strength. Pep talks motivate, but do not transform. Thirty days is a beginning, not an end, and you must begin by inviting Jesus into your journey because He is the great change-maker!

Study Bible)

[4] https://www.instagram.com/30daychangeinme in Highlights and 30daychangeinme.com

so if the son
sets you
free
you will be
free indeed.

John 8:36

IDENTITY

Before we can launch into this journey of transformation thirty days at a time, one element is crucial to understand: your identity.

We often look for freedom in our lives by making lifestyle changes, but the truth is, real change begins with a change of heart.

Heart change doesnt happen by following a prescriptive diet plan or organizing everything in your closet.

Instead, the root of true heart change—the kind that leads to lasting transformation—begins with our beliefs about our identity.

Today, there are many voices out there competing to tell you who you are, who God is, and who you were created to be. Self-help books often suggest that reciting mantras is the road to discovering wealth, success and happiness. The media wants viewers to believe they're one product away from becoming a younger, more beautiful version of themselves, and that this is the way to acceptance and love.

But dear one, I want you to lean in as I tell you a crucial truth:

> *God deeply loves you, and it's only through a relationship with Jesus that you can be made free.*

30-Day Change in Me isn't a self-help book, but rather an "only God can help" book because this journey is not just mental and physical, but also (and most importantly) spiritual. It is going to take a renewal of your mind and a focus on your true identity as God's child to experience the abundant life Jesus promised.

So, before you begin taking on these thirty-day challenges, I want you to take some time to self-examine. Where have you believed a false identity?

Your Voice:
I can't figure it out.

God's Voice:
I will direct your steps.[5]

---

[5] Proverbs 3:5-6

Your Voice:

I'm tired of trying. I just want to give up.

God's Voice:

I will give you strength to keep going.[6] Don't lose heart.[7]

Your Voice:

I can't do it. It's impossible.

God's Voice:

You can do all things.[8] All things are possible with me.[9]

Your Voice:

It's not worth it.

God's Voice:

It will be worth it.[10]

Your Voice:

I'm not able. I'm not smart enough.

God's Voice:

I am able.[11] I will give you wisdom.[12]

---

[6] Isaiah 40:31

[7] 2 Corinthians 4:16-18

[8] Philippians 4:13

[9] Mark 9:23

[10] Romans 8:28

[11] Ephesians 3:20-21

[12] James 1:5

Your Voice:

I am trapped. I've always been this way. I can't change.

God's Voice:

I have set you free.[13] I have made you a new creation.[14] Walk in freedom.[15]

Which voice is the loudest in your life?

Take a moment to identify where your voice is louder than God's voice in your life, and surrender those lies to Jesus.

Lord,

I recognize that I've believed my voice over yours when it comes to my identity. Fill my mind with Your truth, so I can walk boldly into freedom and the abundant life You promised.

Amen.

---

[13] John 8:36

[14] 2 Corinthians 5:17

[15] Psalm 119:45

But seek first
his kingdom and
his righteousness,
and all
these things
will be given to you
as well.

Matthew 6:33

1

CHALLENGE 1: FIRST THINGS FIRST

The What: For the next thirty days, give Jesus the first thirty minutes of your day.

The Why: When you put Jesus first, everything else falls into place. (Matthew 6:33)[16]

The Backstory:

Raise your hand if you're a person that gets easily inspired.

What I mean is, you go to a conference, watch a Netflix show, or listen to a sermon, and you are pumped. The message just resonates in your soul, and you immediately want to spring into action.

The other day I watched the show "Tidying Up

[16] Matthew 6:33: "But seek first his kingdom and his righteousness, and all these things will be given to you as well."

with Marie Kondo,"[17] where an adorable Japanese woman who "loves messes" knocks on people's doors and helps them organize their home for the long term. After a couple of episodes, I was hooked! I desperately needed that organization, and before the next opening credits could roll, I had hit "pause" and said to my husband, "Let's do this!"

I proceeded to throw all the stuff in my closet onto the bed into different piles, then in true "Marie Kondo" style, held up each piece of clothing and asked aloud: "Does this make me happy?" If it did, I kept it; if not, the clothing piece ended up in the giveaway pile.

Often, we want to jump into action at that exact moment of inspiration, and there is a lot of motivation and reason to do so. However, when did you last hit "pause" and take a look at the state of your heart? Before we go boldly into the next decision or sprint off in a new direction, we need to remember our reasons for doing so.

Is this going to lead me to be more like Christ? Does this decision propel me forward into the abundant life Jesus promised?

Am I inviting Him into my messy heart and allowing him to clean out the junk? The things that don't

---

[17] Based on the book by Marie Kondo: The life-changing magic of tidying up: the Japanese art of decluttering and organizing (Berkeley. Ten Speed Press: 2014)

bring Him joy because He knows they're bad for me, or distracting me from His good plan for my life?

FIRST THINGS FIRST

Get your heart right with God. Invite Him into your entire journey—the organized parts of your day, the scattered unpredictable parts of your day, your morning commute, your Starbucks run, your meal planning, your ups, downs, and "all-arounds."

When I lived and taught in Panama as a missionary teacher, there were many ups, downs, all-arounds, and even "turn-arounds." On the teaching side, every day was new, for better or worse. And on the missionary side, it was always an adventure living in spontaneous obedience to what God said to do. There was a lot on my plate, and even though I knew I needed to rely on God, it was easy to live in my own strength.

After one particularly trying day, I remember walking into the school the next morning and seeing the kindergarten teacher had put up a new bulletin board in the hallway.

On it was a poem that forever changed my perspective on inviting God into my day. Read it and ask God what he wants to say to you:

The Difference

By Alan Grant[18]

I got up early one morning
And rushed right into the day;
I had so much to accomplish
That I didn't have time to pray.

Problems just tumbled about me,
And heavier came each task,
"Why doesn't God help me?" I wondered.
He answered, "You didn't ask."

I wanted to see joy and beauty,
But the day toiled on, gray and bleak;
I wondered why God didn't show me.
He said, "But you didn't seek,"

I tried to come into God's presence;
I used all my keys at the lock.
God gently and lovingly chided,
"My child, you didn't knock."

---

[18] Grant, Alan. "The Difference." https://www.amazon.com/Difference-Christian-Art-Inspirational-Metallic/dp/B0778TJ2CZ Visited on 07/01/2019

I woke up early this morning,
And paused before entering the day;
I had so much to accomplish
That I HAD to take time to pray.

When I first attempted these nine #30daychangeinme challenges, I jumped right in with the "Clean Eating" challenge and the other physical challenges.

It wasn't until trying to complete the round of challenges a couple of years later that I realized I needed to flip the order.

We couldn't jump into radical physical change on our own strength. We would never make it for the long term. We might be able to stick to some habits, but our heart posture wouldn't be right. The closet of our hearts would remain cluttered and chaotic by merely adding the Clean Eating challenge, exercise and other physical changes to our already full plate of things to remember and do.

Trying to accomplish all of this on our own would only lead to spiritual and physical exhaustion.

It is mission critical that you intentionally invite Jesus into your day. Give him your first moments, whether that be thirty minutes or an hour. If you're a busy working mom like me, give him your commute and listen to Scripture, or talk to him about your day before the rush begins. He promises you His rest and peace; not that the situations you face will immediately calm down, but you will have HIS perspective when going into these situations.

Psalm 91 promises:

"Whoever dwells in the shelter of the Most High
Will rest in the shadow of the Almighty,"[19]

Notice the order: "dwelling, abiding, living in" comes before "resting, refueling, pausing, finding peace." This verse demonstrates a powerful principle for all of life.

Another critical thing to notice is that sometimes we fill our schedules with DOING things for God versus spending time with Him.

I remember in 2017, during my first months of marriage, my husband and I were fully invested in serving together with our church. It wasn't a bad thing, and we got a great deal of fulfillment out of being able to pour into the next generation and disciple students.

However, I found myself repeatedly using service as a substitute for my daily devotion time. I would justify this switch by saying, "But Lord, I'm spending this time serving you–volunteering as a youth group leader, small

---

[19] Holy Bible: New Living Translation. Wheaton, Illinois: Tyndale House Publishers, 2004. Print.

group leader, church greeter, investing in godly friendships, etc." At the time, I could feel the Spirit tugging on my heart. Jesus was metaphorically standing by the door saying, "I miss you. Come in, sit down, rest, eat with Me. Come back to your first love." (Revelations 2:4; 3:20).

No amount of serving or ministry can substitute for time actually spent with God.

During that year, as I juggled various serving opportunities along with being a full-time high school history teacher and newlywed wife, my lack of time with Jesus began to show. I will admit that, unfortunately, I had become pretty skilled at hiding the weaknesses in my life, making it seem like I had everything together. That's part of the reason why I desire to be completely transparent with you in this 30-Day Change in Me journey. That is to say, pretending can take a lot of work–stuffing emotions, putting on a personality for people, and working hard to balance all the areas of life at once. But I will tell you, friend, that that type of life is completely and utterly exhausting, and eventually, the cracks in that "perfectly" crafted pot will begin to show. And if your pot cracks, and it happens to be hollow, all that's left to leak out is emptiness and darkness.

Those closest to me started to notice first. These

confidants observed that I was slipping into old habits like secret eating, pride, impatience, expressing frustration over little things and changes in my carefully made plans—things that wouldn't have typically thrown me so off-kilter.

I cannot stress this enough. You need a tribe. Those trusted friends that will tie you to a tree so-to-speak, and have that intervention. Those friends that you feel safe with and will care about you enough to tell you the truth. If you don't have these people in your life yet, start praying and asking God to send them, and be that kind of friend to others. Again, that's why we have the #30daychangeinmetribe—so you know you're not in this journey alone. We are there not only to celebrate each other's victories, but also to encourage each other when we fall short to get back up again and face our giants in Jesus' name.

I'm so thankful to have friends and a husband who lovingly yet blatantly speak truth into my life. They said things like, "Hey, this isn't you," and, "I've noticed that lately, you've..." The most shocking to hear was, "You're not acting like Jesus right now."

Often, we need that intimate tribe of people to hold a mirror up to our face and recap our actions like an instant replay tape. I highly recommend you seek out those Christ-following truth-speakers in your life.

For me, after a few interventions from my tribe, I

finally saw what they saw, what the Holy Spirit had been trying to tell me. The reason I hadn't been acting like Jesus was that I hadn't been spending intimate time with him on a daily basis. I had been running around trying to do all the things and be everything to everyone.

Instead, I needed to surrender "all the things" to Jesus. I needed Him to be my everything, my only One.

So I had been trying to pour life-giving water out of my broken pot into my students, church, and family, and all the while my pot had been completely emptied. When the circumstances of life tapped me, only dust shook out. And it was quickly becoming apparent that I was letting the flesh govern my desires and not the Spirit.

At church one Sunday, I had a heart-to-heart with Jesus about it through the worship song, "One Thing Remains."[20]

"Your love never fails. It never gives up. Never runs out on me."

I knelt to the floor by my seat in a physical posture of humility.

---

[20] One Thing Remains (Your Love Never Fails), written by Brian Johnson, Christa Black Gifford, and Jeremy Riddle of Bethel Music Publishing

Lord, I'm sorry. I have been striving in my own power and strength and not relying on You. I'm sorry for not coming to You first. Come and fill me with You. Renew my mind and spirit to follow You and love You first.

I woke up a half-hour early the next morning, committed to giving Jesus the first moments of my day. I sat in the stillness of our apartment balcony overlooking the still-sleeping city, and I opened my Bible to one of my favorites: Psalm 27. My heart resonated with verse 4 (NIV):

"One thing I ask from the Lord,
this only do I seek:
that I may dwell in the house of the Lord
all the days of my life,
to gaze on the beauty of the Lord
and to seek him in his temple."[21]

As I tasted the sweet words of Scripture, I pictured myself sitting next to Jesus as He reassured me of His promises and reminded me of what was important.

After reading Psalms 27, I turned to Galatians 5:13-26, which speaks about walking by the Spirit and the fruits of the Spirit. If you have genuinely made Jesus the Lord and Savior (your #1) in your life, these fruits should

[21] New International Version. [Colorado Springs]: Biblica, 2011.

be evident: love, joy, peace, patience, kindness, goodness, faithfulness, gentleness and self-control. But again, when your pot is empty from being poured out or never having anything poured into it in the first place, you won't ooze the Holy Spirit fruit juice from your cracks.

So first, you need the redemption and healing that Jesus offers. This involves a position of humility on your part, a willingness to be molded by Him and sometimes refined and reshaped in the Word. Then, you need to ask Him to fill you...and I'm not talking just raising your hands on Sunday and singing, "Holy Spirit come."

This deep filling doesn't happen just by listening once a week to a 45-minute message, by socializing with Christian friends, or other ways we look for Jesus. While these things are good and life-giving, they are not your source. These godly activities should be like adding salt to your life; they should make you thirstier for the real thing! The Source of living water!

In John 2:1-11, Jesus transformed ordinary water jars into vessels carrying the best wedding party wine. I believe, in the same way, Jesus can mend our broken pots and transform the stagnant, lukewarm water in them into bubbly "fruit of the Spirit" juice. He makes us effervescent from the inside, spilling over the rim so people can get a taste of Jesus when they're around us.

So how does this authentic filling and transformation take place? One word: Scripture.

Here's what the Bible has to say about itself. Note: This is just a short list. As you read and explore the Bible, I'm sure you are bound to discover more! :

1. It's God's Word: literally Him speaking to you. (2 Timothy 3:16-17)
2. It teaches us how to love God and love others well. (John 14:15; 15:13)
3. It has a purpose: to teach, reprove, correct, train and equip you for every good work (2 Timothy 3:17). Pay attention while you read! Which of these is the Holy Spirit doing in you?
4. It is the source of truth: the Bible grounds you in who God is, who you are, and who you are called to be in Jesus. (John 8:32)
5. You can go to the Bible when you have doubts, and rest in God's perfect character. (Proverbs 30:5)
6. It can be used as a sword against the enemy's attacks. (Ephesians 6:17) Memorize specific scriptures to fight against temptation and defeat the lies in your life.
7. You can go to the Bible for wisdom in making decisions. (James 1:5)
8. It is living and active, meaning there is a fresh word for you each day! (Hebrews 4:12)
9. It is compared to a lamp guiding you in a dark

world. (Psalm 119:105)

10. It is our daily sustenance (bread)... what are we filling up on each day? (Matthew 4:4)
11. It is so powerful that when you speak it, share it, sing it and live it, it changes hearts and lives and creates a ripple effect. (Isaiah 55:11)
12. You are blessed if you hear/read, it and then obey it. (Luke 11:28; James 1:22)
13. If you abide in it, you will know God's will and be able to pray with discernment and power because you are aligning your prayers with God's kingdom purposes. (John 8:31)
14. It is of eternal value. (Isaiah 40:8; Matthew 24:35; 1 Peter 1:23-25)

Now that we know a little bit about what the Bible says about itself, let's dive deeper into studying and applying His Word to our lives.

Remember, it's not about how long you pray or how deeply you study Scripture. It's about your willingness to sit and listen to Him to speak, your desire to be with Him, and creating that space in your schedule just for Him.

Your quiet time with Jesus might look different depending on your season.

It might look like getting up a half-hour early before the kids and sitting with your journal, pen and open Bible. It might look like having your Bible open by your breastfeeding station and instead of watching Netflix, praying scriptures over your sleeping baby and asking God for wisdom in parenting. It might look like sitting in your car during your lunch break and listening to worship music, asking God to speak to your heart. Whatever season you're in, know that God sees you, He loves you and just wants to spend time with you.

If you need some encouragement in this, consider the words of Jesus in Matthew 6, starting in verse 5:

> *"And when you pray, do not be like the hypocrites, for they love to pray standing in the synagogues and on the street corners to be seen by others. Truly, I tell you, they have received their reward in full. But when you pray, go into your room, close the door and pray to your Father, who is unseen. Then, your Father, who sees what is done in secret, will reward you."*[22]

Prayer and Bible study do not have to be elaborate, complicated tasks. Rather, God looks for a *"sincere and contrite heart" (Psalm 51:17),* and *"if you draw near to Him, He will draw near to you" (James 4:8).*

The How

If you can create the space in this season, here are

---

[22] New International Version. [Colorado Springs]: Biblica, 2011.

a few of my favorite methods to get started studying the Bible:

The First Five App (by Proverbs 31 Ministries)[23]

Download the app on your phone/tablet to get daily reminders to spend time in God's Word. Passages are thoughtfully selected, and a short devotional follows. There are also engaging studies on books of the Bible, artistic lock screens with Scripture that you can save to your phone, and a thriving community to join for accountability, prayer and spiritual growth.

PTC: Promise, Truth, Command

Get three highlighters, each in a different color, and designate a color for the following themes: promise, truth, command. As you read, look for these three themes and highlight them accordingly. Then, verse by verse, pray and thank God for His promises, declare His truths over your life and circumstances, and ask Him to help you to follow His commands.

Word Study

Pray and ask God to reveal a character trait or area of your heart that needs to be refined. Listen and watch during the week for any repeated words (sermons,

---

[23] The First Five App was created under the vision of Lysa TerKeurst and the Proverbs31 team in 2015 to help people study the Bible and incorporate time in the Word into their daily lives.

conversations within your godly relationships, songs on the radio, literal signs on the road, etc.) which are "Holy Echoes." Write down this word or phrase, then set aside some solo time, free of distractions. Use a concordance or online tool to look up where this word or phrase is in the Bible.

Have your journal out and write the word/phrase at the top. Write out the Hebrew or Greek definition. Then write down each Bible reference with a quick summary next to it about what you learned about that word or phrase from the verse. After you finish this Scripture/summary list, pray through each summary, asking the Lord to reveal how His Word can transform that area of your life.

SOAP

S-cripture: what are you reading?

O-bservation: what do you notice?

A-pplication: what are you going to do?

P-rayer: invite Jesus into the conversation and your plan of action.

GROW

G-reet: "Good morning, God. Come and teach me today. I want to hear Your voice through Your Word."

R-ead: Open your Bible.

O-bserve: "God, what are you saying to me in your

Word?" Did a particular word or phrase seem to jump off the page?

W-rite: Write down what He's saying to you. Writing it down helps us remember and internalize the message.

FOCUS

F-oundation (read Scripture)

O-bservation (notice details)

C-larification (original meaning)

U-tilization (cross-references)

S-ummation (respond to what you've learned)

The most important part of Scripture study is inviting the Holy Spirit to speak to you.

Note: God wrote the Bible for His children–it's His love letter to them. So truthfully, step #1 is making Jesus your Savior because in doing so, you will become a child of God. Once you have done that, He will allow you to hear His voice more clearly, and you may start to notice specific words jumping off the page at you. He will begin to speak to your heart about every part of your life: relationships, time, priorities, habits, decisions, etc. He will give you ideas, hope, strength and reminders of how to walk in the freedom He's given you. He will show you how to walk by the Spirit, be discerning when it comes to the truth, and accept His grace.

Then and only then will you be able to walk through life with a full pot, and only then can you begin to pour into the lives of others.

Challenge #1: For the next thirty days, give Jesus the first thirty minutes of your day.

Reflection Questions:

1. Are you currently setting aside time and space in your day to meet with Jesus? Realistically, what does this look like for you?
2. Pick a Bible Study method to try this month. Write out what God is teaching you. What does His Word say about who you are, who God is, and what you were created to do?
3. Who can you invite to study the Bible with you?
4. If you don't already know Jesus, I would love to share more about Him with you, and how you can experience new life and freedom. Message me at 30daychangeinme@gmail.com

The prayer of a righteous person is powerful and effective. Elijah was a human being, even as we are. He prayed earnestly that it would not rain, and it did not rain on the land for three and a half years. Again he prayed, and the heavens gave rain, and the earth produced its crops.

James 5:17–18

2

CHALLENGE 2: DRAWING CIRCLES

The What: Pray specifically and consistently over 30 days or until God answers.

The Why: When we pray specifically, God gets the glory!

The Backstory:

In January 2015, I read a book that changed my life. It was *The Circle Maker*[24] by Mark Batterson. Recommended by my prayer warrior friend, Esther Brunat[25], the book is centered around the theme of prayer, and praying with specificity so God gets the glory.

Like most regular church-goers, I grew up with

---

[24] Batterson, Mark. *The Circle Maker*: Praying Circles Around Your Biggest Dreams and Greatest Fears. Zondervan: 2016

[25] Connect with her on Instagram: @estherbrunat

prayer just embedded into my daily routine. We prayed as a family before meals, we prayed to open and close the church service, and we prayed together before bed. It was routine, it was familiar, and I loved it. I always had a long list of people or events to pray for when bedtime came around, just so that I could stay up a little longer than usual. I still remember that my parents placed an *Operation World* flip calendar on the kitchen table starting when I was in fifth grade. I was fascinated, flipping through the pages, learning about the world's different countries, and learning to pray for their needs.

But it wasn't really until college that I had this wake-up call. I was doing all these "religious" things as part of my daily routine, but I saw them as more of a checklist rather than a response to Jesus pursuing me. Jesus began to shift my perspective of prayer and worship as I met people in college from diverse backgrounds and denominations, and I witnessed how there was no one correct way to worship. It was the first time I heard someone pray in tongues, recognized the feeling of the Holy Spirit, and knew in my heart that I was deeply loved and understood.

Yet, when expecting God to do a miracle, I didn't pray with confidence.

If someone was sick, I prayed, "Lord, please give the doctors wisdom."

If someone experienced tragedy, I prayed, "Lord,

give this person comfort."

Then, in my morning devotions, I would read about Jesus doing miracles on the spot. Just look at Matthew chapter 8; you see Jesus healing a leper, a paralyzed man, and Peter's mother-in-law, not to mention calming a storm on the Sea of Galilee and casting out demons. All in one chapter. Whoa.

Was I praying like I believed that Jesus had that kind of authority?

Not really. My prayers tended to be relatively tame, and I could hardly pinpoint if God answered the prayer or not.

But the truth is: Jesus has the power to heal, to redeem situations, to restore relationships, and to bring life out of dead situations.

We don't have because we don't ask. We don't see everyday miracles because we don't seek out these answers or expect God to work in this way. Don't get me wrong; God isn't Oprah, giving away cars right and left to those who "believe."

But God is more powerful than we can fathom, and frequently, we don't give Him credit for answered prayer. His promises are true for us, so we can claim those promises as His children and declare those over our lives. Declaring Scripture has power because we already know that it lines up with God's will for us, and that He will follow through on His promises.

About five years into living and teaching in Latin America, I read Mark Batterson's *The Circle Maker*. The book introduced me to the concept of "praying circles," which involves praying specifically, praying through/over the long haul, praying persistently, praying confidently, and praying over your God-given dreams.[26] (Batterson) In other words, this means praying until you receive an answer, focusing on your prayer target but being humble and open to how God chooses to answer: His best for your life.

> *"Each prayer is like a seed that gets planted in the ground. It disappears for a season, but it eventually bears fruit that blesses future generations. In fact, our prayers bear fruit forever."27*
>
> Mark Batterson, *The Circle Maker*

Forever? I was mesmerized. Do you mean that our prayers last as a legacy for our children, grandchildren and so forth, down the line? We need to get on it!

---

[26] Batterson, Mark. *The Circle Maker*: Praying Circles Around Your Biggest Dreams and Greatest Fears. Zondervan: 2016

[27] Batterson, Mark. *The Circle Maker*: Praying Circles Around Your Biggest Dreams and Greatest Fears. Zondervan: 2016

"What prayers are not being answered because they've just never been asked?"[28]

Mark Batterson, *The Circle Maker*

At the end of the book, Batterson challenges the reader to write a specific list of dreams/goals for the future and begin to pray specifically over them. In that season of my life, I had been living and teaching as a missionary in Panama for four years. I was feeling so satisfied in my work and purpose, yet at the same time, longing for that life partner to serve God right along with me. Honestly, I didn't see many prospects in terms of meeting single Christian guys, though I did try to seek out a Spanish-speaking church in order to meet people outside of my Christian school bubble.

I was seriously considering moving back to the U.S. just because I really wanted to get married when Lisa Patino[29], my mentor at the time, spoke some words of wisdom into my life. We were walking together to our boot camp fitness class, and she said, "You know, Laura, you should start praying for your husband."

I looked at her like she was crazy. How could I pray for someone I didn't even know yet? What would I pray for? But as the afternoon workout got harder, I began to

---

[28] Batterson, Mark. *The Circle Maker*: Praying Circles Around Your Biggest Dreams and Greatest Fears. Zondervan: 2016

[29] Instagram: @lisagpatino

pray between bench presses. I needed strength at that moment, so maybe my future husband did too.

Shortly after, my friend Esther recommended *The Circle Maker* to me, and I knew in my heart this was the space where I needed to write out precisely what I was praying about when it came to my future husband. Sure, like any single Christian girl, I had made many lists in the past of the qualities I desired in a husband. But I had never really invited God into that conversation because I wanted to control that area of my life (which, for the record, does not work).

This list was different. ***I prayed and invited Jesus into the conversation.***

Lord, what do I truly need in a husband? The first thing Jesus showed me was that I needed a man who could remain calm in stressful situations. Then the list went on for about a page, full of qualities that were non-negotiable: a man living the abundant life!

The Husband List:

Someone I highly respect
Life learner
Man of peace
He gets along well with most people
Calming presence, especially in the midst of trials and my freak out moments

Optimistic, willing to laugh, and easy to laugh with
Visionary but very practical, goal-oriented and driven
Natural leader but humble
Gives credit to God always
Serves others before himself
Man of integrity
Pure (motives, experience, internet history)
Loyal
Creative (likes games)
Daily devotions
Soaks in Scripture and quotes it at appropriate times
Financially responsible
Plays an instrument *or loves music
Good cook
Disciplined in eating, exercise, and overall health and spiritual walk
Wants and loves children
Patient and doesn't easily anger
Articulate writer
(Later) enjoys hugging, holding hands (**I taught him to like this)
His job allows him to be present in our family's life, and we have open communication
Patient teacher (new skills)

Interesting eyes
Taller than me *God had me cross this out; it didn't matter. That was because I felt insecure about my height.*
Travels well (has traveled)
Wise, speaks the truth, and affirms others
Seeks mentors and advice
Passionate about similar things (long conversations about the world, events, vision); Committed to God's plan
Self-confident and reassured in his identity in Christ (mentors younger ones; loves discipleship)
Forgives easily

Every morning in my quiet time with the Lord, I would go through my list and ask him to bring that man of God into my life who would become my husband. As I went through my day, certain qualities on that list would resonate in my mind, and I would pray for my future husband, asking God to develop and strengthen these qualities in him. There was no magic formula, just praying specifically and seeking His will in my life. Laying this desire of my heart before Him, I allowed God to prepare my heart for the day that I would meet my husband.

Three months later, I was serving with my youth

group at their annual retreat at Palabra de Vida (Word of Life) camp in Chame, about an hour and a half outside of Panama City, Panama. This handsome guy stood in line behind me for the slackline rope challenge, and he struck up a conversation with me in Spanish. Though he and I spoke in my second language, something about him made me feel like we had met before–something about him that made me feel comfortable to share in Spanish about my life, and sparked a curiosity in me to know more. He introduced himself as Jovanni, and one of the first things Jovanni told me was that he loved to serve people. I was surprised and found this intriguing, as most people don't mention that when introducing themselves. "Serves others before himself" was near the top of my daily prayer list.

Jovanni and I only had the chance to talk briefly as we had to prepare for the next activity, but the rest of the weekend, I watched as he put his words into action. I saw him serving the kids or serving the other adult leaders throughout the camp by cleaning up or helping set up the events. Since I was in charge of the games for the entire retreat, I kept reminding myself that the focus was on the kids, not this kind stranger I had just met.

But Jovanni continued to serve selflessly, and he even helped me clean up all the materials from the camp off the vast soccer field and load them into my car. I was so preoccupied with trying to drive out of the camp before the buses left that I didn't even say thank you or goodbye to him. Nevertheless, on the drive back, my thoughts were spinning. I commented to my friend, Esther, that it was just "so encouraging" to know there are still kind, genuine Christian guys out there.

Fortunately, despite my rude departure, Jovanni pursued me by getting my Facebook information from a friend of mine. We proceeded to message each other during that week (he was traveling outside the country), and he invited me to go for a run together in the park by my house that next Monday.

While we jogged, Jovanni shared with me stories of God answering prayers in miraculous ways in his life and, when I caught my breath, I shared with him about God's faithfulness and how I ended up in Panama as a missionary teacher. Something within my spirit leapt from being around him; the conversation topics he chose were so very near and dear to my heart. The feeling was mutual, and we wanted to keep talking. He treated me to dinner in the nearby plaza, and we had the chance to talk some more.

At one point in the conversation, Jovanni paused, looked me in the eyes, and said, "Laura, I want to be very intentional with you. I'm interested in being your friend, then becoming best friends, then if God wills it, more intimate." I was surprised by his candor, but appreciated his intentionality and care for me.

"Sounds good," I said.

I didn't know how to respond or even what this all meant. I had never had a guy pursue me in this way.

Little did I know that the weeks and months to come were to be the best of my entire life. I would experience friendship and love beyond anything I had never experienced before. I loved getting to know Jovanni's friend group, and appreciated how they demonstrated sacrificial love and served one another. I remember when Jovanni sacrificed his savings to go serve with me on an arduous mission trip to an indigenous village in Ecuador. Not only that, but Jovanni gained rapport with my parents and, incredibly, earned my dad's trust. I will never forget the time when Jovanni scaled my balcony because I had left my apartment gate key inside, or when he surprised me with roses and chocolate when I arrived back in Panama after summer vacation. The examples are numerous, and I'll save the rest for another book.

Long story short, after five months of friendship/best friendship and six months of officially dating, Jovanni proposed to me in a helicopter and completely took my breath away.

On the day of the proposal, I went back and thumbed through the notes I had written in *The Circle Maker*[30], which I had read and prayed through a year

---

[30] Batterson, Mark. *The Circle Maker*: Praying Circles Around Your Biggest Dreams and Greatest Fears. Zondervan: 2012.

earlier. It was both incredible and humbling. Every single criterion I had been praying about for my future husband was met in Jovanni and then some! God knew there were a few things that were superficial that I didn't really need, so He had me cross those out. He also knew there were several things I left out that I actually needed in a spouse, and Jovanni happened to have. Plus, there were a few surprises.

Three weeks after our initial meeting, I gave Jovanni *El Hacedor de Circulos*[31] (*The Circle Maker* in Spanish) as a departing gift when I went to visit California for the summer. We reread it together while we were apart, discussing it over long video calls. While serving on the mission trip in Ecuador, we took time each day to meet and read through *Draw the Circle*[32], a practical guide to praying circles.

I remember being so exhausted from hard labor and lack of oxygen one day, that I collapsed in a field of flowers on a mountainside. I sat looking out at the mountains and began to draw circles in the dirt, praying aloud for different areas of my life, including Jovanni. "Lord, I am really falling for Jovanni, but if this is not

---

[31] Batterson, Mark. *El hacedor de círculos: Cómo rodear de oración nuestros principales anhelos y desafíos (Spanish Edition).* Zondervan: 2012.

[32] Batterson, Mark. *Draw the Circle: The 40 Day Prayer Challenge.* Zondervan: 2012.

from you, I need you to show me." In that same moment that I was praying aloud and surrendering control of the situation, Jovanni came walking up behind me saying, "Laurita, I was looking all over for you."

I blushed as he sat down next to me to take in the scenery, hold hands, and pray together.

What about you?

Do you commit your "prayer circles" to God?

Do you invite Him into the conversation to tell you what you truly need?

1 John 5:14-15[33] says,

> *"And this is the confidence that we have toward him, that if we ask anything according to his will, he hears us. And if we know that he hears us in whatever we ask, we know that we have the requests that we have asked of him."*

We'll save the more in-depth conversations about the mysteries of God's sovereign, moral and permissive will for another day. But the point is this: If we truly believe that God is all-powerful, all present, and all-knowing, why don't we come to Him with our requests?

If you look at the Bible, you will see story after story of people beseeching the Lord. You see answers ranging

---

[33] New International Version. [Colorado Springs]: Biblica, 2011.

from a son being born to a barren woman (ex. Sarah, Hannah, Rebekah, Elizabeth, Samson's mom) to a king seeing his shadow go backwards up the stairs (2 Kings 20).

There are some incredible promises about prayer in the Bible.

Claim these over your prayers and renew your confidence in our good God[34]:

- **Pray with bold faith:**

  "'Have faith in God,' Jesus answered. 'I tell you the truth. If anyone says to this mountain, 'Go, throw yourself into the sea, and does not doubt in his heart but believes *that what he says will happen, it will be done for him. Therefore, I tell you, whatever you ask for in prayer, believe that you have received it, and it will be yours. And when you stand praying, if you hold anything against anyone, forgive him, so that your Father in heaven may forgive you your sins."*

  (Mark 11: 22-25)

- **Pray together:**

  "Again, I tell you that if two of you on earth agree about anything you ask for, it will be done for you by my Father in heaven. For

---

[34] All Scripture quoted below is from: New International Version. [Colorado Springs]: Biblica, 2011.

where two or three come together in my name, there am I with them."

(Matthew 18:19,20)

- **Know that praying makes a difference, and God uses "ordinary" people:**

  "Is any one of you in trouble? He should pray. Is anyone happy? Let him sing songs of praise. Is any one of you sick? He should call the elders of the church to pray over him and anoint him with oil in the name of the Lord. And the prayer offered in faith will make the sick person well; the Lord will raise him up. If he has sinned, he will be forgiven. Therefore, confess your sins to each other and pray for each other so that you may be healed. The prayer of a righteous man is powerful and effective. Elijah was a man just like us. He prayed earnestly that it would not rain, and it did not rain on the land for three and a half years. Again, he prayed, and the heavens gave rain, and the earth produced its crops."

  (James 5:13-18)

- **Pray, even when you don't have the words:**

  "In the same way, the Spirit helps us in our weakness. We do not know what we ought to pray for, but the Spirit himself intercedes for us with groans that words cannot express. And he who searches our hearts knows the

mind of the Spirit, because the Spirit intercedes for the saints in accordance with God's will."

(Romans 8:26-27)

- **Pray, knowing that God is a good Father:**

  "So I say to you: Ask, and it will be given to you; seek and you will find; knock and the door will be opened to you. For everyone who asks receives; he who seeks finds; and to him who knocks, the door will be opened. Which of you fathers, if your son asks for a fish, will give him a snake instead? Or if he asks for an egg, will give him a scorpion? If you then, though you are evil, know how to give good gifts to your children, how much more will your Father in heaven give the Holy Spirit to those who ask him!"

  (Luke 11: 9-13)

These are just a few passages to meditate on as you begin this practice of persistent and specific prayer. As you spend time in Scripture, highlight verses where God speaks to you about prayer and His answers, then turn around and pray those scriptures back to Him.

Celebrate His Answers

Not only is it important to seek God's answers, but it is doubly important that you celebrate His answers. In

Bible times, Israel often set up "standing stones," built altars, composed songs, or renamed towns based on miracles God did. They did this so that their children would remember "The LORD God" was their God and none other.

One way my husband and I commit to doing this is using twelve grapes. In our tradition, every New Year's Eve we take twelve grapes before the clock strikes midnight, and dedicate each of the grapes to a prayer or blessing that we are specifically asking God for in the new year. As we commit each year to Him and ask Him to show off in answering prayer for His glory, we have seen Him answer prayer after prayer. It is always so exciting to watch God answer, whether it be jobs, specific direction, financial provision, our first home, a healthy pregnancy or a stronger marriage. Some requests involve "work" on our part, and we commit those steps of action to the Lord and expect God's breakthrough in those areas of our lives.

Throughout the year, we celebrate Him answering the grapes and, at the end of the year, we go back and check off each "grape" we saw God answer and thank Him specifically for it. We share the news with people we know because what is more exciting than seeing God do an impossible act in your life or experiencing a breakthrough or supernatural provision?!

God continues to answer those specific prayers that

Jovanni and I have prayed for and are still praying for to this day, as we celebrate four years of marriage this year and have welcomed our firstborn son, Benjamin Lou, into the world.

What Happens When God Says No or Not Yet

Though we are encouraged to pray with faith and boldness, sometimes, God in His sovereign wisdom responds with a no. This could be in the form of a rejection letter from your dream company, the guy you've prayed over saying he's not interested, or even a restlessness in your Spirit when it comes to the decision.

"No" is a hard word to swallow. We set our dreams, hopes and plans on this ONE THING to happen. We imagine ourselves in the future living that life, and when we receive the "no" from God, it is heartbreaking. I have often felt frustrated and questioned God's wisdom.

Yet, something happened in the fall of 2018 that has humbled me and taught me to accept it, and have peace when God says no. My husband had been looking for a job for months, when finally it seemed he landed the perfect opportunity. He would earn thousands of dollars in a matter of only a few months of working; the company offered him a brand-new car, a cell phone, free lunch and lodging onsite, health benefits and more. We thought this was the answer to our specific circle prayer for his job.

Jovanni drove three hours down to his training

site, only to find out they had changed the job position. Immediately, he felt unrest about the decision. Though the world would have said he was crazy for not taking this opportunity, he decided to obey the Holy Spirit's prompting to decline the job offer. Our friends and family were baffled by his decision, but he remained firm in his convictions. I knew that my husband listened to God and had an intimate relationship with Him, so I trusted his decision. I told him maybe God had something better planned for him.

Little did we realize that God said no, in order to save Jovanni's life.

Just two weeks after Jovanni declined the offer, he received a barrage of emails from the company because he was still on their employee mailing list.

The e-mail read: "Everybody needs to get out now. Evacuate the area NOW."

A massive fire started in the exact area where Jovanni would have been working had he said yes to the job. This fire was so destructive and uncontrolled in fact, that it wiped out almost an entire town in just a few hours.

Jovanni and I read that email and looked at each other with wide eyes, realizing that God's no and Jovanni's obedience to that answer had literally saved his life.

From then on, when we receive a "no" from the

Lord, we obey. We can't see the whole picture, but God can. And we have to trust His answers even when we don't understand.

Challenge #2: Pray specifically and consistently over 30 days or until God answers.

Reflection Questions:

1. What is something you are praying desperately for God to do in your life or in the lives of others? What are some areas in which you'd like to see a breakthrough?
2. Have you invited Jesus into this area? What is He saying to you about it?
3. What prayers are you afraid to pray?
4. What are some prayers God has answered in your life?
5. What is your prayer life like right now? Other than praying specifically, what ways would you like to improve it?
6. Who can you invite into your prayer journey?

Sing to him,
sing praise
to him;
tell of all
his wonderful
acts.

Psalm 105:2

3

CHALLENGE 3: SONG IN YOUR HEART

The What: For the next thirty days, ask God to put a song in your heart/mind when you wake up.

The Why: God speaks to us in a variety of ways, often through music. Let's take time to listen to what He has to say.

The Backstory:

My whole life, I have loved to sing. I still remember being four years old and singing my very first solo in church. I sang a Steve Green song, "Hide 'Em in Your Heart": "When I am afraid I will trust in you, I will trust in you, I will trust in you. When I am afraid, I will trust in you, my God, whose Word I pray."[35]

[35] Green, Steve. Hide 'Em in Your Heart Vol. 1, 1990. Cassette.

My parents played those scripture song CDs nonstop in the car and the house, and those words stuck. When I was older, I had Scripture embedded in my heart because I had heard the words over and over through song. These scriptures served to encourage me, remind me of my identity in Christ, and allow me to share God's Word with others easily.

I can't overemphasize the role of music in my life and in teaching me biblical truths: from my younger years of Veggie Tales and Steve Green to my teenage years listening to Point of Grace, Plus One, and Relient K. It was such an important part of my spiritual development that, starting in college, when I heard popular songs on the radio that were catchy or had a good melody, I spent time rewriting the words to be about Christ.

Somebody That I Want to Know

(melody "Somebody That I Used to Know" by Gotye; Christmix lyrics by Laura Ortega)

Vs. 1:

Now and then, I think of all the times my life was over
Standing at the edge and wond'ring how far I would fall
But I don't wanna live that way
There's hope and joy in Him you say
All I have to do is let it go
And trust in Jesus...
'Cause He's somebody that I want to know

Short Interlude

Vs. 2:

You can try to be a better person and have peace
But you will never find true joy in the end
Sometimes His grace does not make sense
He opened gates; welcomed us in
Now we are free, and he declares your name

Chorus:
'Cause he gave his life upon the cross
Shed his blood for us when we were lost in our sin
He gave us sacrificial love
From a baby in a manger, though He was God
Why did He have to stoop so low
Send Himself to pay our debt and take on human nature
All my life to Him I owe
That's why He's somebody that I want to know
Somebody (I want to know)
Somebody (Jesus is somebody that I want to know)

Vs. 3:

Now and then, I think how Jesus helped me stand
Firm upon his Word... as I claim His promises
I honor Him with highest praise
'Cause He's the name above all names
I lay down my crown, bow at His throne
Because He is somebody that I choose to know

Chorus 2x:

'Cause he gave his life upon the cross
Shed his blood for us when we were lost in our sin

He gave us sacrificial love
From a baby in a manger, though He was God
Why did He have to stoop so low
Send Himself to pay our debt and take on human nature
All my life to Him I owe
That's why He's somebody that I choose to know
Somebody (I want to know)
Somebody (Jesus is somebody that I choose to know)

I believe music is a powerful venue that God designed for us to meet with Him, praise Him for His goodness, express our heart and create a spirit of gratitude. Now, God still teaches me through secular music, but I know that if I listen to it too much or listen without a discerning heart, my heart and mind will start focusing on the messages of this world rather than on His promises.

If you think about it, music is all around us. It sets the tone. Whether it's the catchy pop music you hear walking down the aisles of Target, or the soft guitar strumming in the background of your favorite coffee shop, music creates the atmosphere.

What would happen if we allowed music to create an atmosphere of worship? In our homes? In our cars? As we shifted the spiritual atmosphere to think about God and His goodness, would we begin to act differently? Treat our children and spouse differently?

Here's what the Bible has to say about music:

- We can use music to share what God has done in our lives.

  Psalm 96:2-3
  "Sing to the Lord, bless his name; tell of his salvation from day to day. Declare his glory among the nations, his marvelous works among all the peoples!"

- We are invited to worship through song together; it's a joyful experience.

  Psalm 95:1
  "Come, let us sing for joy to the Lord, let us shout aloud to the Rock of our Salvation!"

- We can use music to encourage each other with messages from the Spirit.

  Ephesians 5:19
  "...speaking to one another with psalms, hymns, and songs from the Spirit. Sing and make music from your heart to the Lord..."

- Music is a powerful tool to remember specific instances of God's faithfulness.

  Psalm 105:2
  "Sing to him, sing praise to him; tell of all his wonderful acts."

- Music can be used for teaching spiritual truths and

giving thanks.

Colossians 3:16
"Let the message of Christ dwell among you richly as you teach and admonish one another with all wisdom through psalms, hymns, and songs from the Spirit, singing to God with gratitude in your hearts."

According to Overview Bible's website, there are 185 songs in the Bible (150 of them being in Psalms).

Worship Your Way to Victory

The most incredible story to me is in Joshua 6. The Lord is leading Joshua to conquer various cities throughout Canaan that are not following the Lord, to enact justice, and give the land to the Israelites that was promised to them. Jericho was one of the strongest walled cities in the land. Archaeologists say Jericho had a double-wall, complete with a retaining wall and then a mudbrick wall measuring roughly 14 meters (46 feet) high. Because Jericho was well prepared for a siege, they could have held out for months with an ample supply of fresh water and food. But the Lord gave the Israelites victory in just seven days.

The battle strategy is strange, yet Joshua follows the Lord's commands exactly.

Joshua 6: 2-5:

"Then the Lord said to Joshua, 'See, I have delivered Jericho into your hands, along with its king and fighting men. March around the city once with all the armed men. Do this for six days. Have seven priests carry trumpets of rams' horns in front of the ark. On the seventh day, march around the city seven times, with the priests blowing the trumpets, have the whole army give a loud shout; then the wall of the city will collapse, and the army will go up, everyone straight in."36

It's the worship team that marches with the Israelite army. Not only that, but they were carrying the Ark of the Covenant, which symbolized the presence of God. The directions given were purposeful: it was the ultimate prayer walk. On the last day, they were to sound the trumpets. But these trumpets were not the ones used to signal warfare. Instead, they were instructed to sound the trumpets used for celebration and worship. When the seventh day came and the army and priests shouted, they didn't know if the walls would fall–they had to trust and have faith.

And, lo and behold, God did something mind-blowing that final day.

---

[36] New International Version. [Colorado Springs]: Biblica, 2011.

The thick and impenetrable walls of Jericho crumbled to the ground in an instant. The Israelites entered the city by faith, not force.

It's the same in our own lives: we invite the presence of God and circle those areas of our lives where we want God to break down strongholds and set us free. Sometimes we circle these walls in silence, trusting that God has already given us the victory. Sometimes we circle these walls with loud declarations of the freedom to come, and often, God gives us specific instructions to live in the victory He's given us, even after the walls have fallen.

When we worship, we invite God's presence. He renews our minds, reminds us of His goodness, and gives us His peace. When we worship with others, we enter into that unity as His family and prepare our hearts for serving Him together. If you look at the significant victories and breakthroughs in the Bible, worship almost always came first.

In order to enter Canaan, the Israelites had to cross the Jordan River which, at flood stage, was around 100 feet wide. To show that He was with Joshua as He was with Moses, the Lord parted the Jordan so the Israelites could cross on dry land. But the day beforehand, there was a special ceremony where the people cleansed themselves in order to be set apart as God's holy people. They read the Word of the Lord, and they had the Ark of the Covenant pass before them.

> *"Joshua told the people, 'Consecrate yourselves, for tomorrow the Lord will do amazing things among you.'" (Joshua 3:5)*[37]

Worship Through Every Emotion

In the Bible, you see multiple instances where David, before and after he was made King, sang praise to the Lord and helped the people remember God's great works. Yet, a characteristic I admire about David is that he was always honest before God. He also composed songs of lament and frustration. I love this truth: God knows our hearts and wants us to come honestly before Him. Songs of worship don't necessarily have to be joy-filled. In reality, I believe the most powerful worship songs happen when we are facing impossible dilemmas and don't have the answers.

'Tis So Sweet

One of my favorite hymns is "'Tis So Sweet to Trust in Jesus," written by Louisa M.R. Stead. Born in England, Louisa felt the call to missions early in her life, but illness prevented her from going. When she was just a young mom, her family experienced a devastating tragedy. During a family picnic, Louisa's husband heroically dove into the ocean to save a drowning boy,

---

[37] New International Version. [Colorado Springs]: Biblica, 2011.

but the current was too strong, and both the husband and the little boy drowned. Louisa was left alone on the shore, clinging to her 4-year-old daughter, having just watched the unthinkable happen before their eyes.

Following this tragic and unexpected loss of her husband, Louisa grappled with the Lord. Why would He allow this to happen? Was God still good?

Amid the heartache and ensuing destitution, God provided over and over again for Louisa and her daughter's needs. Whether it was the intentional act of kindness from a stranger, or a grocery owner who dropped off food on their doorstep, Louisa was constantly amazed by the miraculous ways God came through during those desperate times. Louisa's daily cry was one word: "Jesus." And He did not fail to answer.

Read the lyrics, listen to the song, and be reminded of our dependence on Him.
In our joyful moments, in our most desperate moments, our song can be "Jesus."

'Tis So Sweet to Trust in Jesus[38]

By Louisa M.R. Stead

Verse 1:
'Tis so sweet to trust in Jesus,
Just to take Him at His Word;
Just to rest upon His promise,
And to know, "Thus saith the Lord!"

Refrain:
Jesus, Jesus, how I trust Him!
How I've proved Him o'er and o'er;
Jesus, Jesus, precious Jesus!
Oh, for grace to trust Him more!

Verse 2:
Oh, how sweet to trust in Jesus,
Just to trust His cleansing blood;
And in simple faith to plunge me
'Neath the healing, cleansing flood!

Verse 3:
Yes, 'tis sweet to trust in Jesus,
Just from sin and self to cease;
Just from Jesus simply taking
Life and rest, and joy and peace.

Verse 4:
I'm so glad I learned to trust Thee,
Precious Jesus, Savior, Friend;
And I know that Thou art with me,
Wilt be with me to the end.

---

[38] Stead, Louisa. "Tis So Sweet to Trust in Jesus." Songs of Triumph. 1882.

When we trust in Jesus, He gives us rest in His promises, healing for our wounded hearts, life and rest and joy and peace, despite the circumstances. He gives us the grace to trust Him more.

Louisa and her daughter ended up moving to South Africa to serve as missionaries; Louisa remarried, and the words of the song she penned were sung by the people they ministered to in present-day Zimbabwe. And now, over 100 years later, her words of worship live on every time we sing her hymn and remember that it is so unbelievably sweet to trust in Jesus.

On a Personal Note

If you have faced heartache or are in the midst of a troubling situation, first of all, I want to send you a hug. I want you to know you are seen, you are loved, and you are not alone.

You may not have the words to say, but the Lord hears your heart. Our whispers through tears are easily understandable by our loving Father–the heartache is familiar to Him as He watched His own innocent Son suffer and die on the cross. Yet, He knows the bigger story. He knows when your "Easter Sunday" will come. There will be justice, there will be redemption. One day, there will be an end to suffering. The light will overcome the darkness.

Even at this very moment, Jesus is worthy of your trust. Lean on Him, process your thoughts and emotions with Him, and find rest in His open arms.

For all of you, I pray these thirty days that you will lean in, listen and ask God to speak to you through song.

Pray and ask God for the songs to face the battles in your life. Sing your way to healing and freedom, and experience Jesus' sweet and unfailing presence.

Challenge 3: For the next thirty days, ask God to put a song in your heart/mind when you wake up.

Reflection Questions:

1. What songs have most impacted your life? Why?
2. What message is God speaking to you through song this month?
3. Take some time to reflect on God's character or promises and write a song to him. (It's okay if you don't have perfect pitch.)
4. Who could you invite to do the song challenge with you?

If anyone is thirsty,
let him come to me
and drink.
He who believes in me,
as the Scriptures said,
'From his innermost
being will flow
rivers of living water.

John 7:37–39

CHALLENGE 4: DRINK UP

The What: For the next thirty days, drink half your body weight in ounces of water each day. Ask God to teach you about the Holy Spirit as His living water.

The Why: This is beneficial not only for our health and wellness, but also to remind ourselves that the Holy Spirit lives in us and fills us.

The Backstory:

Being an elementary, then middle, then high school teacher in Latin America was full of many joys and adventures. But there is one disadvantage to being a teacher that you need to know about: water (or lack thereof).

It's not that you don't have access to water or aren't allowed to bring water to school. It's that you only have four-minute passing periods between classes with a rushed thirty-minute lunch, and you can't just leave the students in the middle of class, saying you have to go to the bathroom.

Not only that, but living in a humid country, you go to work out and you're already sweating. Once I became more disciplined in my weekly workout plan, I knew I needed to adjust my water intake. Embarrassingly, I had to go to the hospital one time for an IV because I was dizzy and nauseous; but now I realize it was most likely because I was dehydrated and didn't know it.

When I moved to California and became an educational consultant, I finally had the freedom and flexibility to use the restroom whenever I needed. Thus, this water challenge was born!

Thirsty

Did you know that when you feel thirsty, you are already dehydrated? The fact is that by the time you feel thirsty, you could have already lost as much as 1 to 3 percent of your body's water content (Mayo Clinic[39]). Dehydration has various side effects like brain fog, stress, headaches, dizziness, fatigue, etc. And your body cannot physically function after three days without water.

---

[39] https://www.mayoclinic.org/want-to-stay-hydrated-drink-before-youre-thirsty/art-20390077

Medical News Today[40] lists several ways your body uses water to function:

- Regulating body temperature
- Helping in the digestive process
- Balancing the pH levels in the body
- Keeping the spinal cord and the joints lubricated
- Creating certain hormones in the brain
- Transporting toxins out of cells
- Eliminating waste
- Transporting oxygen to different parts of the body
- And more!

Who knew that water was so vital to life? Yet we often take it for granted and fail to establish healthy water habits.

Taking the Holy Spirit for Granted

I think in the same way, we often take the Holy Spirit for granted. After Jesus was resurrected, He promised that when he ascended back into Heaven, he wouldn't leave us alone. He sent a Comforter, the third person in the Trinity: The Holy Spirit.

The Holy Spirit's purpose was multifaceted. The

---

[40] https://www.medicalnewstoday.com/articles/290814

Holy Spirit would be a helper to understand God's Word, to prompt us in our daily lives (non-Christians usually refer to this inner voice as your "conscience"), and to advocate for us before God. The Holy Spirit also came to "convict the world concerning sin and righteousness and judgment" (John 16:7-8), to give discernment, and bring people to know Jesus as their Savior. The moment you choose Jesus, the Holy Spirit dwells within you and can give you supernatural wisdom and power, spiritual gifts, and revelation of who God is and what He wants us to do.

But when was the last time you acknowledged the Holy Spirit?

Just like when was the last time you drank 8 cups of water in a single day?

The Holy Spirit longs to fill you with Living Water.

Living Water

This challenge is two-fold because, as you remember to fill up your water bottle, you are also challenged to reflect on the role of the Holy Spirit.

The Bible often refers to the Holy Spirit as "Living Water," but what does that mean? Jesus references this term twice: once in John 4 with the woman at the well, where he mentions but doesn't define the term, and once in John 7:37-39 at the temple.

"If anyone is thirsty, let him come to me and drink. He who believes in me, as the Scriptures said, 'From his innermost being will flow rivers of living water.' But this He spoke of the Spirit, whom those who believed in Him were to receive; for the Spirit was not yet given, because Jesus was not yet glorified."[41]

The Jews at the time would have understood this reference. "Living water" meant water that had a source; water that flowed from a spring or river. People would collect this flowing water in small pools ("mikvehs") where people washed before entering the temple. This ritual purification was mandatory if you ever wanted to step into the temple courts and get anywhere near the presence of God.

Saying these words, Jesus was foreshadowing the indwelling of the Holy Spirit in believers' lives. We would never again have to go through a ritual ceremony of sacrifice or cleansing because Jesus paid the ultimate sacrifice and cleansed us with His blood. We could have an intimate relationship with God. We could have His Spirit living in us, speaking truth to our souls and comforting us, enabling us to comfort others.

Dead Water

In 2018, I had the incredible opportunity to study

[41] New International Version. [Colorado Springs]: Biblica, 2011.

abroad in Israel and Jordan. One of our excursions included a visit to the Dead Sea, on Israel and Jordan's border. The sea has that name because, though the Jordan River flows into it, nothing flows out of it. The water just evaporates, and this leaves behind an incredible amount of salt. Perhaps 37 billion tons of salt!

I was so excited to visit this place. The quantity of salt changes the density of the seawater, which means you can easily float. I envisioned joining the crowds of bobbing tourists in the water, holding books or newspapers without getting them wet. I was so geeked about actually getting to swim in the Dead Sea that I speed-walked down the boardwalk. The glistening turquoise waters contrasted against the crusty salt beach, and I was mesmerized by the beauty of it all. I raised my hand to wave to my friend already bobbing in the water, and at that very moment, my feet slipped out from under me–I found myself sliding full speed down the slippery planks.

Splash! I held my breath, expecting to plunge into deep water, but instead was met with the strangest sensation. My body hit the water in full force, yet I didn't sink or have to struggle to the top. I floated like a rubber ducky tossed into a bubble bath: fin down or fin up, it floats!

Though it was an incredible experience floating in the Dead Sea, I noticed there were no fish in the water.

I'm someone who doesn't like to swim in lakes because you can't see the bottom and identify what mysterious thing is brushing by your legs. So I was relieved to see that no fish were swimming around me.

What was strange is that there were no fish at all! I realized later that hardly anything could survive in the Dead Sea's saline waters, aside from particular types of bacteria and micro-algae. Although the sea provided some gorgeous photos, it was completely and utterly dead.

Let It Flow

My experience there was a powerful spiritual lesson for me. Besides the lesson of "pride comes before the fall," there was the lesson of what happens when we don't allow living water to flow out of us. The Jordan flows into the Dead Sea, but nothing flows out. The water just evaporates, creating an overly salty, dry environment where most living things can't thrive.

What about our lives? Are we drinking deeply of the Holy Spirit and allowing His living water to flow out of us? If we keep it all for ourselves, we will become stagnant and dry. We kill off our ability to live abundantly because we have turned entirely inward, which often leads to selfishness, greed and pride. We think about ourselves, which leads to comparing ourselves to others, which then causes us to hoard our possessions and think more highly of ourselves than we ought. It's a vicious cycle.

Fortunately, if we invite the Holy Spirit to fill us and we are obedient when He gives us opportunities to pour out into the lives of others, there will be a different cycle. We will spend time with God, understand the right perspective of ourselves, and be reassured of His love for us. This revelation of God's deep and unmerited love for us compels us toward acts of love, faith and generosity. We are humbled, willing to give our time and possessions away because we recognize they are gifts from God. As we pour out, He fills us anew, and our lives bear fruit that lasts.

As you drink water this month, reflect on the Holy Spirit and ask God to reveal to you where you can pour out. What difference will experiencing the overflow of this living water make in the lives of people in your circle of influence? In the world?

We were made to be dependent on water for our bodies to function. In the same way, we were made to be dependent on God's presence for the spiritual Body of Christ to function.

John 15:5
"I am the vine; you are the branches. If you remain in me and I in you, you will bear much fruit; apart from me you can do nothing."[42]

---

[42] New International Version. [Colorado Springs]: Biblica, 2011.

Note:

The 30-Day Change in Me Tribe and I recognize that not everyone in the world has access to clean water. In order to pour out and give back, we are partnering with Bridging the Gap 4 Water to raise awareness and build safe water systems in developing countries. Visit their website to learn more! You can donate or start a Walk4Water in your town to raise funds.

Bridging the Gap[43] was started by visionary Shirley Adams, from Chico, California. While hiking to the Mt. Everest basecamp, she crossed seven bridges. God gave her the idea to, "bridge the gap between our country (the U.S.), which has such great wealth, and countries that have so little." God began to give her visions of women carrying containers of water on their heads. She began to pursue the idea further by researching and developing a partnership with World Vision, where 75% of the money raised by Bridging the Gap goes to and is matched by them. All of that money is dedicated to constructing sustainable, clean water systems in West African nations like Uganda and Zambia. World Vision facilitates the crew of local laborers in digging wells and boreholes (hand pumps), and delivering education for the villages on how to use the water system.

Over only eight years, Bridging the Gap has helped

---

[43] https://www.btg4water.org/

to give 17,000+ West Africans access to clean water! I met Shirley Adams a few years ago, and I was inspired by the passion the Lord has given her to pour out into the lives of others. Her Holy Spirit enthusiasm is contagious, and she follows the Lord's direction even if it means biking across the entire United States to raise money for the cause.

Her life is full of living water!

What about you? What evidence is there of living water in your life?

Take these 30 days, and drink up, dear one.

Challenge #4: For the next thirty days, drink half your body weight in ounces of water each day. Ask God to teach you about the Holy Spirit as His living water.

Reflection Questions:

1. How much water do you drink in a day right now? What habits can you establish to incorporate more water into your daily routine?
2. What truth about the Holy Spirit is most powerful for you?
3. Who can you invite to do this water challenge with you?
4. What does it look like for you to pour out "living water" into the lives of others?

Jesus said to them,
"I am the
bread of life; whoever
comes to me shall
not hunger, and
whoever believes in me
shall never thirst.

John 6:35

5

CHALLENGE 5: EAT CLEAN

The What: Eat whole unprocessed foods for 30 days.

The Why: To redeem our relationship with food and discover which foods fuel us.

The Backstory:

I remember it clearly. The half-day I fasted, walked the Cinta Costera–a path bordering the ocean in Panama City, Panama–and had a vision that changed my life. I laid face-down on a bench, praising God and giving thanks, my handy box of tissues just inches from my nose. Then I entered this entirely real movie scene in my mind:

I saw myself sitting on the kitchen floor in my apartment, hand deep into a box of crackers, stuffing my face and crying. Food was my refuge–my safe place and escape when stressed or upset. It was the first thing I reached for when I felt lonely or brokenhearted. My desire for food had gotten out of control through years of overeating (never throwing up), hiding, and even coveting so intensely that it led to broken relationships.

I don't know when it started. It could have been as early as elementary school, when I would wait until no one was home and then sneak a cookie from the cookie jar. It tasted so good, the chocolate melting on my tongue, that I'd go back for another and another. I liked how it felt choosing my food and having no one around to tell me "no." It felt free...that is, until my conscience caught up with me and I realized that it was wrong. I began to feel shameful after the cookie binge, which led to the fear of being discovered. So, I began to hide.

That's the thing about sin. When you choose to rebel and do those things purposefully that you are commanded not to, it's a little addicting, thrilling even, to have this secret way to indulge without accountability or consequences.

The Holy Spirit nudges us not to sin in the first place. Then, it's like warning lights and sirens going off in your mind saying, "Danger. Do not cross."

But choosing to keep on sinning invites the enemy's lies, usually involving his destructive combination of shame and condemnation. If not surrendered to Jesus, these heavy rocks will weigh down your soul. The more rocks you collect, the less you want to admit how many there are. You feel it deep in your stomach: something isn't right. And the lie repeats, "Did God really say...?"[44] The enemy whispers deceitfully that God is holding out on you, not giving you what you want, like a master perpetually holding a bone just out of the dog's reach.

And though you don't want to, you find yourself fantasizing and craving that next opportunity to sin in secret. Pleasure entices you to follow it down what seems to be a beautiful path, but in reality, that road leads to death.

For so long, I justified this overindulgence. It couldn't be sinful! I maintained my holier-than-thou attitude, my pride consuming me as fast as I consumed each and every morsel. Being tall, I could hide the weight gained and often played the comparison game when it came to appearance...I'm not that overweight. Yet this covert sin held me back.

My secret eating reached a breaking point during the year 2010 in my Credential/Master's program. I was spending half the day at the university and half the day student-teaching, and I often wouldn't get home until 7 p.m. I was overloaded with coursework, plus I needed to plan lessons. I felt so overwhelmed by everything that sometimes I just mentally wanted to block out the world

---

[44] Genesis 3:1

and all my responsibilities. I would lay in bed and force myself to go to sleep, or I would go into the kitchen and turn to my old comfort: food. I'd alternate between salty and sweet until my stomach ached, or I ran out of food in the cupboard.

I always felt the Spirit nudging me to stop. Don't do this again! Don't turn there! The sirens were blaring, but I didn't want to listen. I just wanted to feel numb. Of course when I did this, I opened myself up to all the other lies the enemy wanted to throw at me. I unintentionally started to drown out the Spirit's voice with my own justifications and rebellious habits.

Four years later, there I was: stuck. Sure, I had gone on youth retreats where I symbolically buried these sins; I had gone to the altar multiple times in tears wanting to change. I even burned it in a giant bonfire worship service. I had moments where I'd get re-inspired and make an eating plan, and then I'd find myself binge eating again in secret. I even tried Weight Watchers for one summer, and with those changes and accountability, I lost 15 pounds. But it wasn't a lasting change. When I had a frustrating day in the classroom, or when I faced unrequited love and felt that I would never meet someone, I went to the fridge searching.

This wasn't a victory I could achieve on my own. I had dug too deep to rescue myself. I needed a Savior.

February 2015

"Do you believe I am who I say I am?"45

In this vision, it's just Jesus and me in the kitchen together.

"I don't know. This just makes me feel good," I say dismissively, shoveling another handful of crackers in my mouth.

Jesus kneels down beside me on the floor, and I sit with my head in my hands, choking through tears as I swallow. He hands me a glass of water, and I have to drop the crackers back into the box to take it.

"Drink," Jesus says, "I am the living water."[46]

The water is cool, bringing refreshment, and filling my body.

I feel clean again, pure.

Jesus reaches out to embrace me. "I am the bread of life.[47] Eat and be satisfied."

I begin my usual protest. "I know, Jesus. I sing that to you at church, but somehow I can't get my actions to match my words. I am diligent and tracking and staying totally on plan. Then, without realizing what the triggers are–small frustrations, upsets in my plans, the bothersome behavior of others, whatever excuse I can

---

[45] John 14:10

[46] John 4:10

[47] John 6:35

find–I find myself opening the fridge yet again, searching."

"But daughter, what are you looking for?"

I can't avoid His question because I know the answer this time. "I'm looking for satisfaction–a quick fix, an immediate comfort. It's an addiction. I just can't stop." My eyes fill with tears again, ashamed.

"Come to me,[48]" He says, standing to his feet.

I find myself echoing the words of the lame man at the pool of Bethesda[49], always full of excuses. "I can't get up, Jesus. It's too hard. I've been fighting this for too long."

He smiles softly. "It's never too late to come to me.[50] You're not meant to do this by yourself. Give up the fight because I've already won.[51]"

He extends his hand, and I see the nail scars on His wrists. It takes all the resolve within me to fight, and keep on fighting the inner desire to turn away, to stay where I am and sit in this comfortable place. I know that if I take His hand, if I go to Him, it will mean radical change. It will mean giving up what I think is precious: my "drug of choice," and "addictions" which actually held me in bondage for so many years. I turn toward

---

[48] Matthew 11:28

[49] See John 5

[50] Joel 2:12-13 MSG

[51] John 16:33

Him and grab hold of His hand. He pulls me to my feet with no effort.

> *"I am everything you need. I forgive you. You are mine, and no one, nothing can separate you from my love52. I have called you, I have won your battle, and you are free.53"*

When I emerged from this vision, I was free. I was no longer in bondage to food! Did I still have to fight temptation? Sure, but was I enslaved to it? No.

Those of you who face similar struggles or have overcome addiction in the past know that living in freedom does not come naturally. We're so used to these destructive habits that we often not only have to radically overhaul our daily routines, but we have to overturn our old ways of thinking altogether. The truth is, our sinful habits always begin with a thought.

James 1:14-15 lays out the formula for sin:

> *"But each person is tempted when he is lured and enticed by his own desire. Then desire when it has conceived gives birth to sin, and sin, when it is fully grown, brings forth death."*

---

[52] Romans 8:35

[53] John 8:36

But we have a choice. Choice 1 is to entertain these thoughts, fantasizing and idealizing how much pleasure, prestige or pride we will get from doing this one thing this one time.

We know Choice 1 is wrong. We may even feel the Holy Spirit prompting us not to make that choice, but instead of listening we tend to justify whatever emotion we feel, or lie that we want to believe in that moment. Then we proceed to push aside the Spirit and go ahead with our selfish desires. After we ignore the promptings of the Spirit and act on Choice 1, we feel the waves of guilt, but proceed to push them aside and repeat the think-fantasize-act-guilt cycle. It can become a vicious cycle, and the more it's repeated, the more difficult it becomes to discern the Holy Spirit's advice. One of the saddest consequences of continuing to live a life of sin is that God's voice is put on mute.

But what if you made Choice 2? When you're hit with a thought you know could lead you down that road to death, immediately give it to Jesus. In 2 Corinthians 10:5 and Romans 12:21, Paul describes it as "taking every thought captive to Christ." I imagine a slingshot connected to my head. When a sinful thought comes my way, I grab it as quickly as I can and launch it in my slingshot up toward Jesus. He captures that thought and puts it behind bars so it can't distract me from living in the freedom He intended for me to have.

When the temptation pulls harder, remember God is faithful. He will never allow you to be tempted beyond what you can bear. Plus, He promises to provide a way out. (1 Corinthians 10:13) Look for that way out, whether that means physically walking away, finding a healthier way to deal with stress, or sticking to your meal plan.

So what does living in freedom look like?

> *Living in freedom is a daily fight to renew your mind with God's Truth about your identity and your purpose.*

Clean Eating

This time, when I approached a healthy meal plan, I chose to invite Jesus. I joined friends on a Clean Eating plan where you focus on whole foods for thirty days and eliminate added sugar, dairy, grains, legumes, soy, carrageenan, MSG and sulfites. It was one of the most difficult challenges I have faced (besides exercise, but we'll get to that later) for several reasons: a) it seems everything in the store has some sort of added sugar in it, b) the act of saying no and committing to a meal plan for real was new for me, and c) it took a lot of time and intentionality.

On the "Clean Eating" regimen, your body reacts differently depending on how much processed food you were eating before. In the beginning, you might experience drowsiness, bloating and intense cravings, but a little beyond midway through you experience a crazy amount of energy. I noticed I slept better, had clearer skin, and didn't have that after-lunch energy slump like I usually did. When the "Clean Eating" challenge is over, you can slowly reintroduce foods into your diet, and that's when you realize how certain foods affect you. For example, I discovered that sugar gives me headaches, and bread makes me feel tired.

Despite the challenges, my friends and I made it through the 30 days. We didn't experience any dramatic weight loss, though we did slim down some.

The real gains from our month of "Clean Eating" were:

A. Mindset - I CAN commit to eating well and having self-control.
B. Creativity - Who knew all the recipes you could make with sweet potatoes?
C. Health - There are so many benefits, like having energy I didn't have before.
D. Camaraderie - There's a bond that forms when you achieve something difficult with your friends.

Since that first "Clean Eating" challenge month, I've completed three additional "Clean Eating" challenges at times in my life when I needed that reset.

Establishing exercise routines also motivated me to eat for fuel and not so carelessly. Today, I have a healthy relationship with food and enjoy it as a gift, but don't look to it as my god.

When I feel tempted to slip into old habits, I remember Jesus freed me. He opened the door to my self-made prison and shined a light on all my dark corners. I'm not forced to stay here; I have the choice every day to walk out the door and live in freedom.

But sweet friend, know that living in freedom is a choice. To do so, I have to be vigilant, arming myself with Scripture, prayer and good friends.

Because, although the battle has been won, I'm still in the fight.

Challenge #5: Eat whole, unprocessed foods for 30 days.

Reflection Questions:

1. What area of your life have you been fighting to find freedom in? Do you have a source of temporary comfort (like food) that is not God? What are you searching for when you give in to temptation?
2. What does the Bible say about the addiction you have, and God's ability to set you free?
3. Does anyone know about the struggle you have? If not, talk to someone you trust.
4. Take a more in-depth look at who Jesus says He is. In what ways specifically does He satisfy your search?
5. What is your relationship with food?
6. What is your "why" when it comes to this challenge?
7. Who could you invite to join you in this challenge?

For the moment all
discipline seems painful
rather than pleasant, but
later it yields
the peaceful fruit of
righteousness to those who
have been trained by it.

Hebrews 12:11

6

CHALLENGE 6: EXERCISE

The What: Be intentional to exercise (break a sweat) at least thirty minutes every day for thirty days.

The Why: Exercise is not just good for the body, but good for the spirit. Exercise can be a spiritual discipline.

The Backstory:

Exercise. That dreaded word makes me shudder. The word that makes you think back to running laps in middle school, the track with the hill, the gym teachers appropriately named "The Monster." It's the one word that dredges up feelings of resistance even before you start–always something you were forced to do and hated.

I was the kid whose very last option was to choose to go outside and play. I spent hours in imaginary play, dreaming up stories with my dollhouse people or reading through the entire American Girl doll series in one sitting. My parents enrolled me in soccer in second grade, but I spent the season talking with other kids or wandering around the field. I only ran out of necessity...that is, if the ball came anywhere near me. I considered it a successful game if I was able to keep as far away from the ball as possible. After all, I hated running, and I quit after that fall season.

In eighth grade, my dad patiently prepped me to try out for the middle school basketball team. I idolized the girls in their cool basketball uniforms and matching hair scrunchies like a secret club I wanted to be a part of. I don't think I even liked basketball—I just saw the potential to get to know these cool girls and figured the running would be good for me.

I remember scanning the lists after tryouts: first the A-team, then the B-team, then the C-team. I walked away disheartened. I had practiced so much, and I didn't make any of the teams, not even the C-team! I came to the sad conclusion that I may have been tall but, with no coordination whatsoever, I wasn't meant to ball.

Transitioning to high school, I finally found that camaraderie I had longed for when I joined the marching band. In fact, I stuck with it for all four years, but let me tell you...marching band takes multitasking and coordination skills to the max. From remembering where your dot is on the field, to maintaining correct form/posture, and memorizing complicated musical pieces, it's a workout for both the body and the mind. Not to mention you have to remember to breathe. I was in a sport for the very first time! We even got to travel and compete, and we won the State Championship in our category two years in a row! But even after surviving hot summers of marching on asphalt at band camp, I still didn't love exercise.

And I never thought I would.

That is, until my freshman year of college at Westmont. Set in the foothills of Santa Barbara, framed on one side by mountains and the other by the ocean, it was an idyllic place to fall in love with the outdoors. We'd have study parties on our dorm lawns, and walking to class usually involved a trek up the hill.

During my first semester, I had to take this class called Fitness for Life. I cringed when I saw that on my schedule. It reminded me of the phrase on the gym clothes we had to wear in high school: "fit for life." I soon learned it was a class that served as an introduction to health and fitness, required for my elementary education major, and complete with its own set of physical measurements and tests.

But one test was on my mind the most. We would

be given a semester-long assignment based on this one task: running the mile.

Of course, I was a painfully slow runner and had to walk some parts in the end, gasping for air as I pushed myself to jog across the finish line. Fifteen minutes. A girl who walked every lap finished close behind me. I couldn't believe how slow I was, and I knew what that time meant.

It meant I had to complete and log at least 30 minutes of exercise for four days every week that semester. Now, though I may have been lazy with exercise, I was not a slacker when it came to academics. Fortunately for me, I wasn't the only one in the class facing this dilemma. I overheard the girl who walked the entire thing voicing the same complaints I was rehearsing in my head.

"Hey, I have four days too! Do you want to do the workouts together?" I asked, and she agreed. So I gained a workout buddy in Kristin, and the days and weeks that followed turned out to be a learning experience and a blessing in disguise.

A) I realized I'm a social exerciser–the time goes by much faster when talking between laps with a friend.

B) Exercise is a spiritual discipline.

Running laps became a focused prayer time with Jesus. Sure, most of the time, it was breath prayers like "help me, Jesus" or "give me strength." At other times though, I was able to rehearse and memorize Scripture, enjoy His creation, give Him any weighty worries, and wrestle through my thoughts with Him by my side.

Sometimes, I imagined Jesus pushing me from behind, giving me that spurt of energy to sprint to the finish line. In other moments, I pictured Him as my coach running ahead of me, showing me how to run and what path to take, encouraging me to press on and not give up. Most often though, I envisioned Jesus running by my side.

He had run this race before, and this time, He ran as a friend and confidant. He empathized with every painful intake of air or cramp forming in my side.

> *He knew the struggle times a thousand, and He knew me so intimately that He chose to run alongside me. This way, we could finish the race together.*

Honestly, the second realization–that exercise was not just a health need but a spiritual discipline–changed my perspective of exercise forever. I began an exercise routine in my twenties of trying to run three times a week. While living and teaching in Honduras, I joined fellow teachers for a weekly running club. I also joined my super motivated roommates in learning how to follow exercise videos like 30dayshred[54] or Taebo[55]. Incorporating exercise two to three times a week definitely boosted my energy, but I couldn't "outrun my fork," as people say. My eating habits didn't match my exercise efforts, so I didn't see any dramatic results.

When I moved to Panama in 2012 for a different teaching position, I joined an exercise boot camp in the school parking lot every Tuesday and Thursday. The boot camp used a combination of step workouts, weight/resistance training, and circuit training. It was led by none other than Coach Jimmy, a well-known local personal trainer.

Jimmy, a burly yet kindhearted man, offered these boot camp classes for free as a ministry of the church and school. Jimmy was a dedicated coach, coming over to examine and correct your form or giving you a heavier band to make the movement more challenging. Thirty or so women and I would sweat it out together in Panama's humid weather twice a week. Jimmy led us through a complicated step routine, complete with weights and bands set to his playlist of '80s music, and pushed us to the limit. Sometimes he'd look around so proud of us. He'd grab someone's water bottle and drip it on his face saying, "Is that a tear? I'm crying. You guys are doing so well." He was always full of one-liners like that, and

[54] Created by Jillian Michaels

[55] Created by Billy Blanks

though we were sore, we smiled under the sweat and kept coming back for more. Even I became a regular.

My exercise routine changed dramatically when I started to date my future husband, Jovanni. Establishing a more fit lifestyle was something we both wanted for ourselves, so we hired online husband and wife coaches: Parker and Ashley. The couple provided us with a complete workout plan and eating plan. (The eating plan was another way that I got my eating under control and started to live in food freedom.) Due in part to the fact that I was motivated by the chance to see Jovanni, and also because Jovanni had a gym in his apartment building, I became the most consistent I had ever been with a lifestyle fitness plan. And slowly but surely, I began to see results.

In fact, I was down thirty-two pounds from my highest weight (195) when I was in the throes of an intense MEd program at UCSB seven years prior. As I prepared to say my forever yes in marriage to the man I had fallen madly in love with, I weighed in at my lowest: 163! But again, the most significant transformation was on the inside. The me in 2016 would have trouble recognizing the me in 2009. Sure, I still loved Jesus, but in 2016 I was experiencing a level of freedom and love I had never felt before. I actually began a pattern of turning to Jesus instead of food or sleep, and began to deal with my emotional immaturity and past struggles with self-esteem.

I began to rest in the truth: I was and am fearfully and wonderfully made. (Psalm 139:14) God gave me this body as a temple[56], so why had I been trashing it for so long? I was done making excuses, justifying my laziness and overindulgence, and done lying to myself that this was something I could overcome on my own. I needed Jesus.

I needed Him right then in the same way that I needed him in the past. The same way I needed him:

- When I hit my lowest moment during my student teaching and He showed me His rainbow. I broke down crying, realizing He saw me.
- When I had to push against fear and return to finish my credential program. God so abundantly provided and helped me to succeed, renewing my passion for teaching.
- When I was teaching in Honduras and my student's father was shot in front of him. I had to tell him that his dad died, even though he had prayed for God to save him. This unexpected tragedy led to a heartbreaking yet beautiful moment where I was able to share about Jesus' sacrifice and love with my fourth-grade class.
- When my closest teacher friends left Panama and

---

[56] 1 Corinthians 6:19-20

I was left lonely and questioning who would be around me. A year later, God provided me with the people at Panama International Church, my now-husband Jovanni, and his loyal friends. This tight-knit community became more of a family than I've ever known a church family to be.

I needed Jesus to push through the hard things, to rely on His supernatural strength and power when I couldn't see what was ahead, and to ease my mind when I was in doubt. I needed Jesus in my exercise routine and in my eating plan. I needed him running to push me from behind, running in front of me, and most importantly, running beside me.

So I invite you now to take on this challenge, inviting Jesus alongside you the whole way.

The How:

Here are a few tips in order to complete the 30 days of exercise challenge:

1. Find an exercise plan you enjoy! Maybe you are a social exerciser like me and want to join a Zumba class, or maybe you do best hitting the track just you and your EarPods. You will more likely stick with it if you enjoy it!
2. Fit in the appropriate time or incorporate it into your daily routine. Are you an early bird? Then wake up at 5 a.m. before anyone else in the house

and get that workout in! Or maybe it feels best for you to come home from work, throw your workout clothes on and get your exercise in before dinner. Be realistic about how long you have to work out (30 min is the goal, but you may work up to it).

3. Plan ahead. Will you work out at a gym or at home? If you choose to work out at home, what will you need–weights, mat, towel, water bottle? Set a clear space and communicate with others so they respect that space during your exercise time.
4. Know yourself and what your body can handle. You can build the strength and endurance, but give yourself that time. Pace yourself, drink water, fuel yourself with good food during the day, and slow down/modify exercises. Rest if you need to.
5. Remember, the focus isn't weight loss; the focus is developing healthy habits that help your body feel its best and help you have the energy to live the abundant life.
6. Switch it up! Monotony leads to boredom, and boredom often causes us to quit. Get creative, ask your friends or the 30-Day Change in Me Tribe, and discover new ways to exercise!

And most importantly...

Wherever you are in your fitness journey, whatever programs or exercise videos or gyms you've tried or haven't tried, have you invited Jesus to join you?

Challenge 6: Be intentional to exercise (break a sweat) at least thirty minutes every day for thirty days.

Reflection Questions:

1. What's your backstory when it comes to exercise?
2. What does following an exercise program for thirty days look like to you? What is your game plan?
3. What is your biggest fear or obstacle when approaching this challenge?
4. What exercise activity, video or regimen are you going to follow?
5. What are three benefits you hope to gain from exercising?
6. As you exercise, write down the times you've felt Jesus close by.
7. What friend can you invite to do the 30-day exercise challenge together?

Therefore, as God's chosen people, holy and dearly loved, clothe yourselves with compassion, kindness, humility, gentleness, and patience. Bear with each other and forgive one another if any of you has a grievance against someone. Forgive as the Lord forgave you. And over all these virtues put on love, which binds them all together in perfect unity

Colossians 3:12–14

7

CHALLENGE 7: FASHION

The What: Take a picture of your outfit for thirty days and share the images on your social media with the hashtag #30daychangeinme.

The Why: How we present ourselves affects how and if our message is heard.

Preface

So now that you've pushed through two hard lifestyle changes, it's time for something a bit more lighthearted–but something we definitely need to devote at least thirty days to improve, and that is: FASHION.

As I thought about this fashion challenge at the outset, I realized it was so much more than just putting together "Instagrammable" outfits and capturing that perfect square photo. Since fashion determines how we present ourselves, I found it to be a crucial topic of discussion for us as Christ-followers because we are His representatives.

Have you ever been to a conference where the presenter is incredibly poised, well-prepared and well-spoken, but their clothes are a mess or poorly chosen for their body type? You find yourself easily getting distracted and, at the end of their twenty-minute talk, you realize you weren't listening at all?

Unfortunately appearances do matter, especially if you want your message to get across. And as followers of Christ, we have the most important message out there: the Gospel! What if our clothes (either immodest or poorly chosen) were to get in the way of communicating our message?

The other "why" behind the fashion challenge, and why we are posting on social media is to provide a way to get to know YOU as you share your unique self and encourage the exchange of ideas. We can both teach and learn a lot from each other, from the unsaid rules of fashion and differing definitions, to unique perspectives and personal experiences. In the end, we can mostly agree on what looks best on a person and what colors highlight their best features. So, we're all here to help!

The Backstory:

Here's my fashion story.

Growing up in the '90s, I wore a steady rotation of

leggings and home-sewn sundresses. When my fashion-forward mom introduced me to jeans in the fifth grade, I hated them! (I also used to be someone who hated change–go figure!) I thought jeans were stiff and uncomfortable and vowed I would never wear them. However, I would thank my mom come seventh grade as jeans were pretty much all I wore and still wear today. I am so grateful for my mom's insight and all those shopping trips together. Even so, I was fairly oblivious to the fashion trends pretty much into my college years. Having spent summers on mission trips or working as a camp counselor, I held on to my baggy cargo shorts and old t-shirts.

Fortunately, another fashion mentor entered my life when I met my future husband, Jovanni. It was his friend, Veni[57]. Veni explained to me some significant cultural differences I was overlooking when it came to my fashion choices. Although in the U.S., it was socially acceptable to leave your house without makeup, wear workout pants, and go to the grocery store, in Venezuela where Jovanni was raised, women took great pride in their appearance. It was important that they look "put together" and "made up" at all times.

Well, Veni was just the mentor I needed to propel me from experimenting with fashion and makeup to actually knowing what I was doing. She patiently gave me

---

[57] Connect with Veni on Instagram: @veniuska

makeup classes, showed me what outfits looked best on me, and helped expand my wardrobe to include some "young" outfits–not just what I wore as a teacher. And you know what? When I dressed well and used the right amount of makeup, I felt more beautiful than I ever had before in my life. I also saw how Jovanni's eyes lit up when he saw me. I walked with a new sense of confidence in my identity as God's daughter–beautiful, chosen, and purposeful.

In turn, these changes in makeup and fashion encouraged me on my quest to exercise and eat right, and gave me more clout in my teaching job. Others noticed the difference and affirmed me as a professional; students tended to respect me more when I dressed in my fitted suit jacket and matching shoes. It might have been in my mind, but I learned to leverage my wardrobe on especially trying teaching days and found I became a more firm and consistent teacher.

Based on these experiences, I believe your clothes and the way you choose to dress have an impact on your life as a whole in three crucial ways:

How you feel about yourself.

When you wear those jeans that fit you perfectly or that jumper that highlights your best features, you look in the mirror and smile a little bigger. You feel more awake, alive and ready for the day. In my job, when I put together a professional outfit, I find I can deliver more effective presentations because I see myself as a professional and dress the part. Your outfit of the day helps define your persona as you speak eloquently, field questions and leave your audience thinking.

Did you know that there is scientific proof that there is a connection between what we wear and how we feel about ourselves? It's called: "Enclothed Cognition." Enclothed Cognition refers to the effect that wearing certain clothes has on our feelings, attitudes, self-esteem, and interactions with others.

Because society assigns symbolic meaning to particular clothes (example: suit = powerful, smart, successful), we have these same ideas in our brains when we wear them and tend to act that way. That's why when we put on workout clothes, we are more likely to actually work out because we are already in that mentality.

To demonstrate this, the scientists conducted an experiment.[58] In it, they had two groups of people: Group A wore their regular clothes, and Group B wore their regular clothes, plus they were given lab coats to wear. When both groups took a cognitive performance test, Group B, wearing their lab coats, did significantly better than Group A. The same results were found when both groups were given lab coats to wear, but Group A was told they were wearing an artist's smock rather than a

---

[58] https://youtu.be/MtPPaCBJdw0

doctor's lab coat, as told to Group B.

Because of these associations that we make between types of clothing and specific roles, we evaluate people's clothes often based on the occasion. Society says we need to dress nicer for church on Christmas and Easter because that is just an expectation. If you see someone dressed in sweats with uncombed hair, they may receive judgmental looks because they do not follow society's expectations.

The social psychologist Gauri Sarda-Joshi, writes on the website "Brain Fodder" the following statement about enclothed cognition:

"There's a reason tailored jackets are associated with being 'dressed for success.' It seems that wearing formal office wear and structured clothes puts us in the right frame of mind to conduct business. Wearing power clothing makes us more confident [possibly because we call it power clothing] and even increases hormones needed to display dominance. This, in turn, helps us become better negotiators and abstract thinkers."[59]

But Gauri warns that if you wear formal business clothes for casual events, you will tend to be more guarded and less relational, which is why businesses often implement casual Fridays to boost positive company culture.

---

[59] https://brainfodder.org/psychology-clothes-enclothed-cognition

What impact can this knowledge of "Enclothed Cognition" have on our Christian walk?

We can not only be intentional to dress with excellence for our jobs (Colossians 3:23) and dress in a way that is respectful to others (Romans 14:13 and 1 Corinthians 8:9), but we can remember how we are truly dressed.

> Isaiah 61:10
> *"I delight greatly in the LORD; my soul rejoices in my God. For he has clothed me with garments of salvation and arrayed me in a robe of his righteousness, as a bridegroom adorns his head like a priest, and as a bride adorns herself with her jewels."*[60]

This verse speaks about the year of the Lord's favor regarding Israel, but how favored are YOU? So much so, that Jesus gave His life for you and made it possible for you to experience freedom and the abundant life in your relationship with God. So try waking up tomorrow morning and, while you're getting dressed, instead of criticizing yourself in the mirror, look at your reflection and say, "Jesus has given me garments of salvation and a robe of righteousness."

How would this change your perspective of yourself if you remembered your "robe of righteousness"

---

[60] Isaiah 61:10

throughout the day? Would you treat others with more patience and generosity? Would you carry yourself with more confidence? Would you be able to stand firm in the face of insults because you knew the truth about your identity?

Now that you are aware that how you dress can subconsciously affect how you act, practice choosing your clothes wisely in order to guard your heart.

> Proverbs 4:23
> *"Above all else, guard your heart, for everything you do flows from it."*

In Christian circles, we tend to focus on men and women dressing modestly, so the opposite sex doesn't lust after them. The truth is women don't have control over men's thoughts or sin patterns; no more than men have control over women's thoughts or sin patterns. But men and women can choose to live in obedience to the Holy Spirit. If the Holy Spirit convicts you or prompts you not to wear something, listen.

How others see you

Whether it be a significant other or another important person in your life, their opinion of you matters–their words, whether you like it or not, play a role in how you carry yourself. Have you noticed when you compliment someone on their outfit, their face immediately brightens? They might even treat you nicer than before as well.

It's strange but true. People like to be told they look good.

As Christians our focus is not on making us look good, but on making Christ look good.

These verses explain how we make Christ look good:

1 Corinthians 6:20
For you were bought with a price. So, glorify God in your body.

Colossians 3 talks about putting on your "new self"; your new identity in Christ:

"Therefore, as God's chosen people, holy and dearly loved, clothe yourselves with compassion, kindness, humility, gentleness, and patience. Bear with each other and forgive one another if any of you has a grievance against someone. Forgive as the Lord forgave you. And over all these virtues put on love, which binds them all together in perfect unity."

The Bible mentions that people will recognize we follow Jesus by our love for one another (John 13:35), and by the spiritual fruit we produce (Galatians 5:22). Our spiritual clothing can reflect Christ and protect us in spiritual battles (see Ephesians 6:10-20).

How others hear you

Remember, the majority of what we want to say is communicated before we even say a word. When someone walks into the room, people quickly analyze them (often subconsciously) and rank them. These superficial judgments and comparisons are unfortunate but true. That is why James warns so strongly against favoritism (James 2:1-13).

> *"My brothers and sisters, believers in our glorious Lord Jesus Christ must not show favoritism. Suppose a man comes into your meeting wearing a gold ring and fine clothes, and a poor man in filthy old clothes also comes in. If you show special attention to the man wearing fine clothes and say, 'Here's a good seat for you,' but say to the poor man, 'You stand there' or 'Sit on the floor by my feet,' have you not discriminated among yourselves and become judges with evil thoughts?" (read James 2:1-13 for the full story)*

It is so easy to show partiality or bias. So we need to be conscious of this when interacting with others.

For ourselves though, we can reflect on our fashion choices as a large part of our non-verbal communication.

In 2010, the Swiss bank UBS published an employee handbook laying out explicit instructions for how the bankers should dress, and even some self-care tips.

It was 44 pages long!

Three key statements the UBS made were:

- *"A flawless appearance can bring inner peace and a sense of security."*
- *"Adopting impeccable behavior extends to impeccable presentation."*
- *"The garment is a critical form of non-verbal communication." (UBS)*[61]

I wonder what people think when they enter that bank...do they trust the bankers more with their money because of how they present themselves?

What about with us?

Do people trust us with our message?

We wouldn't want our clothes to negatively affect our ability to communicate the gospel.

Did you know you can even use your clothes to reach others for Christ?

Yes! Hudson Taylor sailed to China in the late

---

[61]https://www.businessinsider.com/ubs-dresscode-clothes-bank-2010-12

1800s as a missionary. After spending time there, he felt so burdened by the Lord for the multitudes of Chinese people that were dying without knowing Christ that he returned to England and recruited even more missionaries to return with him. His outreach strategy? Dress like the Chinese and speak Chinese. At the time, British missionaries mostly hung out with other British workers there and didn't socialize much with the Chinese; they spoke through translators and didn't venture into China's interior. However, Hudson Taylor was convicted. Unless he (and other missionaries) dressed like the Chinese and spoke their language, the Chinese would never understand the gospel or accept its message.

The other Protestant missionaries criticized Taylor for acting in this way. Yet Taylor persisted, and little churches began to form as more Chinese people accepted Christ. When his original mission agency couldn't sponsor him anymore, Taylor branched out and created his own: the China Inland Mission (CIM), known today as the Overseas Missionary Fellowship. Not only did he train in medicine, but he translated the Bible into Mandarin and wrote a pivotal book to convince people in England of China's need for missionaries.

Every year, Taylor prayed fervently for more people to reach the interior of China for Christ. And every year, God answered and exceeded his requests, providing more than the number of people he needed. Everyone he sent needed to dress in Chinese attire. Taylor had the foresight at that time to understand that to dress like someone from another culture means you are seeking to learn more about them, that you respect them, that your status is not higher or better than theirs, and that you want to connect.

Often when it comes to other cultures, elements and ideas are incorporated in fashion today for just that purpose: to connect and celebrate that culture. We also have to be careful to be respectful of those cultures in our own fashion choices.

I learned this the hard way. When I visited Japan in 2008 to volunteer at an international school, I had a very limited view of Japan and its culture. I wanted to dress in "Asian" style, like the cartoons I saw on TV growing up, so I put my hair up in a bun one day and stuck two chopsticks in the bun forming an x-shape. As I was helping in a 2nd-grade classroom that day, one of the little Japanese girls came up to me and pointed to my bun asking, "Why do you have chopsticks in your hair?" I realized at that moment that it must have been like putting a fork and a knife in my hair! Since then, I have learned to seek understanding in my travels and ask a local if it's okay to wear something from that culture or if it will be disrespectful. Never let stereotypes or television guide you in dressing like a certain culture.

The How

Though fashion takes many forms, here are some

general guidelines that seem to work for most people.

1. Dress for your body shape. As Christ-followers, we can dress attractively and modestly. Our clothes can be fitted to our body shape, yet shouldn't be so tight that they are revealing. Remember that you are sending a message, and you want to set a positive example for others. Follow your convictions, and don't compromise.

2. Evaluate your closet. What combinations of clothes do you already have to make outfits? What are you missing? Or, is it time to sell/donate your wardrobe and plan out a shopping trip to build your new closet? If you're looking to minimize the amount of clothes in your closet, and love every outfit in there, investigate building a "capsule wardrobe."[62]

3. Women: Experiment with accessories, shoes, makeup and hairstyles.

   Men: Experiment with ties, belts and shoes.

4. There are many resources out there to help with fashion, even to help you match or create outfits.

---

[62] The term "capsule wardrobe" came from London boutique owner Susie Faux and was popularized by American designer Donna Karan. A capsule wardrobe is basically reducing your closet down to a few pieces of clothing that won't go out of style, and combine to make multiple outfits.

Find an app, community or mentor that can give you feedback and help you dress to feel comfortable and confident in your skin.

What message is your fashion sending to the world?

Challenge 7: Take a picture of your outfit for thirty days and share the images on your social media with the hashtag #30daychangeinme.

Reflection Questions:

1. Reflect on your current fashion choices: How do you feel about yourself wearing this? How do others see you? How are others hearing you? Would you feel comfortable representing Christ in your current wardrobe?
2. What does being "fashionable" mean to you?
3. What are your body type, preferred style, and budget?
4. Who can be your "Veni" and mentor you in the area of fashion?
5. Who can you invite to join this fashion challenge with you?

For God
is not a God of
disorder
but of peace.

1 Corinthians 14:33

CHALLENGE 8: ORGANIZATION

The What: Pick three areas of your living space. Organize them, and keep them organized for thirty days straight.

The Why: Defeat the lie that you're not organized and create useful systems to save time, minimize stress and foster a hospitable home and peaceful marriage/relationships. Develop mindful habits that will help you over the long-term.

Preface

It's time to work on another topic I like to avoid: organization.

For some of you (i.e. Jovanni), this challenge won't be difficult, so I encourage you to reach out to others who are in need of some tips and tricks. Those of us who are creative multitaskers with a full social agenda struggle sometimes with these minor details, such as where we last left our keys.

The Backstory:

The need for an organization challenge came to light during the fashion challenge last month. When I was organized (you know, actually hanging up my clothes in the closet or prepping my outfit the night before), I had a much calmer morning the next day.

Knowing I needed help, I reached out to my husband Jovanni for advice. I am forever grateful to Jovanni's mother for instilling in him a desire (or mandate) for order and cleanliness from an early age. Living in a house with three older brothers, Jovanni knew he had a responsibility to help take care of the home, and his mom scheduled an all-family cleaning day every fifteen days.

I, on the other hand, was a more go-with-the-flow kind of kid. If my room was not clean, I'd just shut the door. Once I realized I could earn stickers on a sticker chart for cleaning up, I became a bit more intentional with putting things away by at least stuffing them inside a drawer where no one could see them. I didn't dislike cleaning...I just had so many other things I wanted to be doing. If only I had known then what I know now, that cleaning as I went would have saved me more time in the end to do the things I wanted to do. I wouldn't have wasted so much time searching for that "lost" item when

I had "put it in a special place" and then forgotten where I stashed it.

I guess I became okay at it because my younger brother once paid me his share of the allowance to clean his room too. I mastered the quick fix cleaning method which consisted of, "Quick! Throw it in a drawer. You can figure out later where it belongs." But of course, I never did.

I remember one negative effect of my disorganization in middle school. I was in seventh grade, and to this day I can't remember what exactly happened. I was always trying to be a good student. Still, there were two major assignments that year that I totally blanked on until the deadline. Between serving in student leadership with the church youth group, figuring out social groups and so on, I couldn't keep my materials or classes straight.

Fortunately my teachers were understanding and showed me undeserved grace, allowing me to make up the assignments. Best of all, my mom intervened to teach me her golden solution to disorganization: create systems! She bought me color-coded notebooks based on each subject, and corresponding colored folders. She helped me cover my textbooks in matching stretchy book covers and labeled everything with my name. English was yellow, science was green, social studies was blue, math was red, and health/physical education was purple.

Amazingly the system worked, and to this day, whenever I enter a new space I try to set up systems to help me stay organized. In fact, I hand-decorated all my binders for my college classes–again, organized by color.

My dad played his part in teaching me organizational skills as well. A social butterfly and dreamer type like me, my dad understood my struggle firsthand. He taught me tricks that helped him, like numbering each of his pockets, having designated spots in the house where he always put things, and remembering how tasks like cleaning up were one particular way that made my mom feel loved.

Now let's jump from middle school to the ripe age of twenty-seven, when I was newly married to the man of my dreams. A few months into my marriage to the amazing Jovanni, I noticed a bit of tension building. We had been trying to merge our lives into one, but somehow we overlooked the fact that we had very different lifestyles and upbringings. We shared a two-bedroom apartment in a Panama City high-rise, and I hadn't established any systems yet. Jovanni and I had an honest conversation and discussed our expectations of one another. The following Saturday, Jovanni joined me in helping me set up these systems. We raised the bed using bed-risers and stored less commonly used clothes and shoes in plastic bins underneath. We committed to a mostly clear shelf space, and Jovanni walked me through his quick and preferable method of folding clothes. Over the short time we've been married, I've seen how when I'm organized, mindful and careful of our space, it not only leads to a calmer feeling in the home but frees up our time to spend it enjoying each other!

Respecting Their Space

Maybe you're married to your "opposite" or they are your roommate/housemate, and you tend to clash over messes. Have those honest conversations with them about your space. I had a powerful "lightbulb moment" the other day when I was in a marriage Bible study, and the woman leading it shared about how men feel respected. One of the ways she mentioned was "their space." I had never thought about that before! How we care for our common areas and respect our spouse's space can affect our marriage dynamics.

For example, I will clear off the counters at the end of the day, usually by sticking things in drawers or trying to find where the items belong. However, I tend to have a short-term memory of where I put things. So when my husband asks me where so-and-so thing is, I draw a blank. "Um...I put it somewhere." He teases me about this, knowing I will begin listing off places where the missing thing could be because I don't want to seem completely clueless. After I stumble through my list and try to rack my brain for where I last saw that thing, my husband usually says, "So, do you know where it is, or are you just guessing?" He already knows my answer. I am still learning not to move his things without telling him where I put them in order to respect his space because at least one of us should be able to remember!

Identity Crisis

Remember at the beginning of the book, I wrote to you about the importance of identity in tackling these 30-day challenges.

Well, you can see based on my backstory that I defined myself as "messy and disorganized" for most of my life. But when I took on this challenge of 30 days of organization, I began to develop a new perspective of myself. It wasn't that I lacked organizational skills; it's that I just never took the time to be mindful and consistent with organizational systems.

1 Corinthians 14:33 says:

"For God is not a God of disorder but of peace."

Here Paul is talking about having order in the church service, but gives us a nugget of truth about God's character. From the way God created the world, to how He keeps it running, to how He arranges time and space to fulfill His purpose, He is a God of order.

God is also a God of peace. So if we strive to reflect Christ, then we want to establish habits that lead to peace. If we're going to establish patterns of organization, it will take some investment of our time and energy, but ultimately it will lead to more peace in our homes.

1 Corinthians 15: 58 says:

"Therefore, my beloved brothers (and sisters), be steadfast, immovable, always abounding in the work of the Lord, knowing that in the Lord, your labor is not in vain."

Learning to be organized takes investment, but the time and energy you spend on this are not in vain!

Also, there is a promise that if you are faithful in these little things, He will continue to entrust you with more (Luke 16:10).

The How

Here are a few organization tips to get you started:

1. Designate a specific place for things, and create easy to use systems in those places to organize the space. Give everything a "home." Here are some suggestions for systems to use:
    - Use drawer dividers: separate kitchen utensils, office supplies, kids' clothes, etc. It helps to see everything you have laid out and sorted into categories.
    - Store items in clear bins or cloth boxes: perfect for separating your winter clothes from your summer clothes, storing toys or books when not in use, or organizing

your fridge so you actually know what to buy at the grocery store.
- Label your bins/boxes: the visual reminder of what goes inside is so helpful.

2. Follow your systems:
   - Take that extra minute and hang up the shirt instead of throwing it in your closet. You'll be grateful later when you want to wear that shirt again and need to find it.
   - Clean as you go. It helps me to divide the house into five zones: eating zone (kitchen/dining area), laundry zone (laundry room), living zone (living/family rooms), sleeping zone (bedrooms), and bath zone (bathrooms). I try to walk each zone before bed and just quickly clear spaces, putting things back where they go, so that the next day, my family is more at peace knowing where they can find items in the morning. The laundry zone and eating zone need constant upkeep since I'm in those zones the most.
3. Declutter: Believe it or not, it is easier to stay organized when you have less stuff! My husband and I try to embed checkpoints throughout our year, when we reevaluate our stuff and sell/give

away/throw away things that we never use or have stopped using. Decluttering is an excellent spiritual discipline as well because it helps us focus on our family versus our stuff, and creates a more peaceful environment. We like the idea of minimalism–saving time, space and money. Someday I think we'll get there. I always tell people that I don't want gifts, I want experiences!

4. Get professional help: There are incredible people out there that call themselves "professional organizers." No really, this is a thing. They will come to your house and organize your spaces. They will guide you through what to get rid of and what to keep. They will help you set up systems based on your lifestyle. I've never had one of these people come to my house, but if it's something you want to invest in as a priority, these people know what they're doing. If not, reach out to the 30-Day Change in Me community and check out our social media for more great ideas to get and stay organized.

Join me in inviting peace into your home, whether you are single, newlywed, or many years into marriage. The atmosphere you set, the time you take will be rewarded.

Challenge #8: Pick three areas of your living space. Organize them, and keep them organized for thirty days straight.

Reflection Questions:

1. Do you consider yourself naturally more organized or a more "go with the flow" kind of person?
2. Are there any lies you've been believing about your relationship with organization or order?
3. How could being more organized change your life and your family's life?
4. What are some systems that work well for you?
5. Who could you invite to join you in this Organization Challenge?

Do nothing out of selfish ambition or vain conceit. Rather, in humility value others above yourselves..

Philippians 2:3

9

CHALLENGE 9: BEING PUNCTUAL

The What: For thirty days, keep your promises to yourself and others when it comes to being on time.

The Why: Maintaining this consistency fosters respect, reputation and trust, and this will flow into every area of your life.

The Backstory:

I never appreciated the art of waiting until I spent eight years living and working in Central America. Unlike North American culture, time and efficiency are not a priority there...instead, Latinos place precedence on relationships.

Though I have grown to appreciate these cultural differences and embrace them, I still remember my frustration and impatience early on. I remember standing in line at the teacher store my first week in Panama, watching as the clerk took each item out of my cart one by one to scan them. Then I needed to stand in yet another line where another person was in charge of bagging the items. Finally, another person stood by the door to check that the receipt matched each item in my cart. It took so much time, and my brain was racing with ideas on simplifying and streamlining the process.

It wasn't until much later that I started to see the beauty in the waiting. For one, there's more opportunity for interaction with the people around you who are also waiting. Second, you have a chance just to breathe and thank Jesus. Living in Latin America has taught me to slow my pace, especially when meeting people. Instead of rushing off with my Starbucks order, I can take time to savor the sacred moments with a good friend at a local cafe.

The other international teachers and I always joked that errands in Panama were considered a success if you accomplished at least two things on your list. Between city traffic, crowded shopping malls, tropical rainstorms, technology malfunctions, language barriers, and navigating foreign territory, it was necessary to always build in extra hours for these unexpected waiting times you'd encounter during the day. So being late to anything other than work became a low priority on my list. Even when I lived in the U.S., friends tended to expect that I'd arrive ten minutes or so after the time we had set together. Living in Panama, I finally had a legitimate excuse for arriving late that everyone would understand.

However, my whole perspective of time shifted in 2015 when I met my future husband, Jovanni. One of the areas where Jovanni and I differed was our perception of time and the importance of being on time. As you have seen in my previous backstories, I'm a very right-brained thinker, always juggling many priorities. To-do lists are frequently on my mind, and in process. If I could have it my way, I'd live without a watch or calendar and just go with the flow.

On the other hand, my husband feels that arriving on time should be extremely high on the priority list. For that reason, he is always aware of the time. He has this unique ability to balance his time and correctly estimate the time needed to get ready, travel and arrive at the next destination.

Thus, I began years of radical reform and struggling to get my scatter-brained self, organized enough to arrive on time.

Here's what I've learned:

- Stay organized: Most of the times when I'm late, it's because when I have everything ready to go, suddenly I can't find my keys or sunglasses. I know I need systems, and I try to build them into my daily routine. (Hence our covering Chapter 8 on organization prior to time management!)

- Keep to-do lists with time estimates. These lists serve three purposes: a) they help organize scattered thoughts, b) they allow you to check off what you need to do in the order you need to do it in, and c) they help you develop a realistic schedule and be more aware of the time.
- Plan and think ahead. If I plan my outfit the night before, I can have a calmer and more efficient morning before work. If I plan my meals and meal prep for the coming week on the weekend, I'm much more likely to stick to my plan (like "Clean Eating") and not be stressed about meals. Build in buffer time and resist hitting that snooze button!
- Set your car clock ahead by ten minutes.
- Keep a time/pace keeper close by, such as your timer on your phone, your very timely husband, or a close friend whom you know is skilled at managing their time.

Time is often people's most precious resource. Yet in the English language, it seems time gets the most negative connotations. We waste time, spend time, we're running around trying to make up for lost time, and time flies by us. It seems we're always running out of time.

So if we decide to be "on time" for others and "on time" for ourselves, we honor people's time and show them they are important to us. People respect and trust you more for arriving on time every time because they can see you are consistent and worthy of their trust. Your reputation for being timely and following through on your commitments opens up more doors of opportunity as you are given more responsibility, and your relationships become stronger. On the contrary, if you are late all the time, it communicates that you are disorganized and irresponsible.

What does the Bible say about this?

Well, there is no commandment saying "thou shalt be on time," but there are other hints of God's expectations of us throughout the scriptures.

Listen to this in Ephesians 5:15-17:

> *"So, then, be careful how you live. Do not be unwise but wise, making the best use of your time because the times are evil. Therefore, do not be foolish, but understand what the Lord's will is."*

Colossians 4:5 says,

> *"Behave wisely toward outsiders, making the best use of your time."*

Multiple times in Scripture, it mentions that our lives are but a breath, that we don't know when our last day on earth is, and so it is crucial that we use our time in a way that glorifies God and helps others get to know Him. We should love others in deed and in truth. (1 John 3:17-18) That involves honoring them, showing they are loved and valued, and having integrity in everything we do.

What about you?

What difference would being "on time" make in your life and the lives of others around you?

Challenge 9: For thirty days, keep your promises to yourself and others when it comes to being on time.

Reflection Questions:

1. Do you tend to be on time, early, or late? Why do you think so?
2. In what areas of your life do you break promises to yourself or others in the area of time? 3. Are there ways you waste time? How could you better use this time?
3. Who could you invite to help you stay accountable or develop good time-saving habits?

the one
who calls you
is faithful
and he will
do it.

1 Thessalonians 5:24

10

CHALLENGE 10: REFLECT

Congratulations, friend! You did it!

You completed nine thirty-day challenges in pursuit of living the abundant life God promised! That's 270 days—almost a full year of challenging yourself and growing spiritually, physically and mentally.

It has been an incredible journey walking through these challenges with you and learning from each other along the way.

But the challenges don't end here. Take this last set of thirty days to reflect and journal about these nine challenges.

Which ones were the hardest to accomplish? Did you still push through?

____

____

____

____

Which ones were the easiest to complete?

____

____

____

____

What did you learn about your ability to help others in that area?

____

____

____

____

What were some truths you learned about yourself along the way?

Are there challenges you accomplished that you want to make a part of your daily routine for longer than 30 days, or for life?

How has your relationship with God changed as a result of these challenges?

My prayer for you is that completing these challenges and reading my story has helped you grow in your relationship with Jesus, and brought you into a new level of freedom and abundant living.

I pray it brought about a new awareness to the areas of your heart that Jesus is asking you to surrender to Him on a daily basis. My prayer is that you can walk in that freedom and surrender, and likewise help others discover that same joy and deliverance in Jesus' name.

Remember, this is not about self-help, but "only God can help," and what He promises to do, He is faithful and He will do it.

John 10:10b (NIV, emphasis added)

"I have come that they may have life and have it ABUNDANTLY."

1 Thessalonians 5:24 (NIV)

"The one who calls you is faithful, and he will do it."

NOTES & SCRIPTURE

The Launch

1. *Holy Bible: New Living Translation*. Wheaton, Illinois: Tyndale House Publishers, 2004. Print.
2. *ESV Study Bible: English Standard Version.* Wheaton, Illinois: Crossway Bibles, 2007. Print
3. John 10:10: "I came that they may have life and have it abundantly." (ESV Study Bible)
4. https://www.instagram.com/30daychangeinme in Highlights and 30daychangeinme.com

Identity

*All scripture links go to: www.biblegateway.com

1. Proverbs 3:5-6
2. Isaiah 40:31
3. 2 Corinthians 4:16-18
4. Philippians 4:13
5. Mark 9:23
6. Romans 8:28

7. Ephesians 3:20-21
8. James 1:5
9. John 8:36
10. 2 Corinthians 5:17
11. Psalm 119:45

Challenge 1: First Things First

*All scripture links go to: www.biblegateway.com

1. (Matthew 6:33)
2. Kondo, Marie. *The life-changing magic of tidying up: the Japanese art of decluttering and organizing.* Berkeley. Ten Speed Press: 2014.
3. Grant, Alan. "The Difference." https://www.amazon.com/Difference-Christian-Art-Inspirational-Metallic/dp/B0778TJ2CZ Visited on 07/01/2019
4. *One Thing Remains (Your Love Never Fails),* written by Brian Johnson, Christa Black Gifford, and Jeremy Riddle of Bethel Music Publishing
5. *New International Version.* [Colorado Springs]: Biblica, 2011.
6. (Revelations 2:4; 3:20)
7. (Psalm 27:4)
8. (Galatians 5:13-26)
9. (John 2:1-11)
10. (2 Timothy 3:16-17)
11. (John 14:15; 15:13)
12. (2 Timothy 3:17).

13. (John 8:32)
14. (Proverbs 30:5)
15. (Ephesians 6:17)
16. (James 1:5)
17. (Hebrews 4:12)
18. (Psalm 119:105)
19. (Matthew 4:4)
20. (Isaiah 55:11)
21. (Luke 11:28; James 1:22)
22. (John 8:31)
23. *New International Version.* [Colorado Springs]: Biblica, 2011.
24. (Psalm 51:17)
25. (James 4:8).
26. https://first5.org/ The First Five App was created under the vision of Lysa TerKeurst and the Proverbs31 team in 2015 to help people study the Bible and incorporate time in the Word into their daily lives.

Challenge 2: Drawing Circles

1. Batterson, Mark. *The Circle Maker: Praying Circles Around Your Biggest Dreams and Greatest Fears.* Zondervan: 2012.
2. https://www.operationworld.org/prayer-calendar
3. Instagram: @estherbrunat
4. https://www.biblegateway.com/passage/?search=Matthew%208&version=NIV

5. Instagram: @lisagpatino
6. https://pdvpanama.org/
7. Batterson, Mark. *El hacedor de círculos: Cómo rodear de oración nuestros principales anhelos y desafíos (Spanish Edition).* Zondervan: 2012.
8. Batterson, Mark. *Draw the Circle: The 40 Day Prayer Challenge.* Zondervan: 2012.
9. 1 John 5:14-15 *New International Version.* [Colorado Springs]: Biblica, 2011.
10. Mark 11:22-25
11. Matthew 18:19-20
12. James 5:13-18
13. Romans 8:26-27
14. Luke 11:9-13
15. Numbers 23:19

Challenge 3: Song in Your Heart

1. Green, Steve. Hide Em in Your Heart Vol. 1, 1990. Cassette.
2. Psalm 96:2-3
3. Psalm 95:1
4. Ephesians 5:19
5. Psalm 105:2
6. Colossians 3:16
7. https://overviewbible.com/
8. Joshua 6
9. Joshua 3:5

10. Stead, Louisa. *"Tis So Sweet to Trust in Jesus." Songs of Triumph.* 1882.

Challenge 4: Drink Up

1. https://www.mayoclinic.org/want-to-stay-hydrated-drink-before-youre-thirsty/art-20390077
2. https://www.medicalnewstoday.com/articles/290814
3. John 16:7-8
4. John 4
5. John 7:37-39
6. John 15:5

Challenge 5: Eat Clean

1. Genesis 3:1
2. John 14:10
3. John 4:10
4. John 6:35
5. Matthew 11:28
6. See John 5
7. Joel 2:12-13 MSG
8. John 16:33
9. Romans 8:35
10. John 8:36
11. James 1:14-15
12. 2 Corinthians 10:5
13. Romans 12:21,

14. 1 Corinthians 10:13

Challenge 6: Exercise

1. *30dayshred* created by Jillian Michaels; *Taebo* created by Billy Blanks
2. Psalm 139:14
3. 1 Corinthians 6:19-20

Challenge 7: Fashion

1. Instagram: @veniuska
2. Experiment video: https://youtu.be/MtPPaCBJdw0
3. Brainfodder site: https://brainfodder.org/psychology-clothes-enclothed-cognition
4. Colossians 3:23
5. Romans 14:13 and 1 Corinthians 8:9
6. Isaiah 61:10
7. Proverbs 4:23
8. 1 Corinthians 6:20
9. Colossians 3
10. John 13:35
11. Galatians 5:22
12. Ephesians 6:10-20
13. James 2:1-13
14. https://www.businessinsider.com/ubs-dresscode-clothes-bank-2010-12
15. The term "capsule wardrobe" came from London

boutique owner Susie Faux, and was popularized by American designer Donna Karan. A capsule wardrobe is basically reducing your closet down to a few pieces of clothing that won't go out of style, which combine to make multiple outfits.

Challenge 8: Organization

1. 1 Corinthians 14:33
2. 1 Corinthians 15: 58
3. Luke 16:10

Challenge 9: Being On Time

1. Ephesians 5:15-17
2. Colossians 4:5
3. 1 John 3:17-18

Challenge 10: Reflect

1. John 10:10b
2. 1 Thessalonians 5:24

A NOTE OF THANKS

Thank you ultimately to my Savior and Lord, Jesus Christ. Apart from You, I can do nothing. Only YOU can transform lives, and the pages of this book are a testimony to Your mercy and love.

Also, I wouldn't be where I am without my tribe–those mentioned in Challenge 1 and throughout this book.

To my Tribe at Home:

Jovanni: My love, thank you for inspiring me to be better every day and for encouraging me to finish what I started.

Benjamin Lou: My baby and my biggest WHY.

To my original #30daychangeinme Tribe:

Thank you for taking on each challenge and sharing your stories! You continue to amaze me with how you are still incorporating what you learned from each challenge to live the abundant life!

To the Tribe who raised my husband and me:

To my parents, Lou and Shirley Diaz, who taught me many lessons, but most importantly modeled for me spiritual discipline and an intimate relationship with Jesus Christ.

To Jovanni's parents, Leila and Enrique Carvajal, who raised Jovanni to be a wonderful husband and father.

To my fifth-grade teacher Mr. Declute, and my mentor, Jessica Meldrum, who both played a pivotal role in developing a love for writing in me.

Special credits to my original tribe:

Veniuska de Cabareda, Rosangelica de Cabareda, and Leidimar Constable.

To my production tribe:

To my Editors, Abbey Espinoza and Lindsey Duffy, thank you for investing your time and talent to give me honest feedback about my book. Your prayerful comments and personal perspective made this book infinitely better!

To my book Interior designers Lorena Nuñez for the beautiful Scripture designs and my book interior designer Md Waheduzzaman Manik who completely captured my vision!

To my Cover Designer, Les germancreative thank you for catching my vision and designing such a professional masterpiece. Seeing the cover was the first time I saw myself as a published author. I look forward to partnering with you in the future.

ABOUT THE AUTHOR

LAURA ORTEGA currently lives in North Texas with her incredible husband Jovanni, and their son, Benjamin Lou. They love to serve at their church and travel in their free time.

Prior to landing in Texas, she spent eight years living and teaching in Latin America as a missionary teacher. She continues to reach the nations through working as an ESL Newcomer Instructional Specialist. God gave her this project in 2018 and, after nine months of completing the challenges, told her to stop and write. This book was completed in 2020 and is a testimony to God's abundant faithfulness in her life.

Connect with Laura:

Instagram: @30daychangeinme

Email: 30daychangeinme@gmail.com

Join the 30-Day Change in Me Tribe!

Find Camaraderie, Community, and Christ as we complete the 9 thirty-day challenges together!

https://www.facebook.com/30daychangeinmetribe
Code to join: BOOK1010

Visit 30daychangeinme.com for more!

30 Day
Change in Me
MINISTRIES

Made in the USA
Coppell, TX
02 April 2021

52984421R00089